CONCILIUM

concilium

1996/6

THE HOLY RUSSIAN CHURCH AND WESTERN CHRISTIANITY

Edited by
Giuseppe Alberigo and Oscar Beozzo
with Georgy Zyablitsev

SCM Press · London
Orbis Books · Maryknoll

Published by SCM Press Ltd, 9–17 St Albans Place, London N1
and by Orbis Books, Maryknoll, NY 10545

Copyright © Stichting Concilium

All the translations in this issue are by John Bowden, with profound thanks to Ann Shukman for her help.

English translations © 1996 SCM Press Ltd and Orbis Books, Maryknoll

All rights reserved. No part of this publication may be reproduced, stored in a retrieval system, or transmitted, in any form or by any means, electronic, mechanical, photocopying or otherwise, without the prior written permission of Stichting Concilium, Prins Bernhardstraat 2 6521 A B Nijmegen. The Netherlands

ISBN: 0 334 03041 2 (UK)
ISBN: 1 57075 075 0 (USA)

Typeset at The Spartan Press Ltd, Lymington, Hants
Printed by Biddles, Guildford and King's Lynn

Concilium Published February, April, June, October, December.

Contents

Editorial GIUSEPPE ALBERIGO and OSCAR BEOZZO	vii
The Significance of the Baptism of Rus' in the Development of Russian Culture D. M. SHAKHOVSKOI	1
The Three Romes EMMANUEL LANNE	10
I· The Faith in Russia	**19**
The Primacy of Monastic Spirituality VLADIMIR KOTELNIKOV	21
The Theological Conceptions of the Slavophiles ALEKSI I. OSIPOV	33
The Experience of the Russian Orthodox Church during the Soviet Regime ADRIANO ROCCUCCI	49
The Fruitfulness and Contradictions of the Russian Emigration NICOLAS LOSSKY	66
II· *Via à vis* the West: Approach and Rejection	**73**
Ecumenical Relations with the Orthodox Churches of the East from a Viennese Perspective FRANZ KÖNIG	75
Between Ostpolitik and Ecumenism ALBERTO MELLONI	89
The Ecumenical Problem in the Russian Orthodox Church in Relation to the 1994 Synod GEORGY ZYABLITSEV	101
Eastern Catholic Churches and Uniatism ÉTIENNE FOUILLOUX	110

The Measures taken by the Moscow Patriarchate between
    1990 and 1992 to settle the Interconfessional Conflict in West
    Ukraine
        GEORGY ZYABLITSEV   118
The Second Vatican Council and its Significance for the
    Russian Orthodox Church
        VITALY BOROVOI   130
Towards a Common Future?
        GIUSEPPE ALBERIGO   143

Contributors   158

To the Readers of *Concilium*. A Statement from the Foundation   162

Editorial

Despite everything, Russia and the Russian Orthodox Church continue to be to a large degree an 'unknown planet' for the West. Even *Concilium* is no exception. This is the first time that, after more than thirty years, our readers have been offered information and reflection on Russian Orthodoxy and its relations with the Western churches.

We have been involved in disseminating knowledge of the 'Third World', the South of the planet, the feminist world, and Christian traditions other than that of Roman Catholicism, but Slavonic and above all Russian Christianity has remained unknown.

This has been the result of the long segregation caused by the Soviet regime and – with it – the anti-Communist ideology which has been dominant on both sides of the Atlantic. In the West two generations have been brought up in the conviction that in Russia Communism has wiped out Christianity. Perhaps even today it is hard to convince people of the importance and the depth of the Christian tradition which is alive and flourishing in Russia, where it has never become extinct.

The preparation of this issue has been particularly difficult, not least because of this situation. It has above all been hard to obtain Russian voices which can give an account of the situation and experience of Orthodox Christianity in Russia from within. With a good deal of difficulty it has been possible to have a number of Russian contributors, but not as many as we would have liked. In this climate it has not been possible to introduce other points of view – as would have been desirable – than those of theologians and churchmen formally committed to the Patriarchate of Moscow.

However, it should be noted that the articles by D.M.Shakhovskoi, V.A.Kotelnikov, A.Osipov, G.Zyablitsev and V.Borovoi, involved in various academic and ecclesiastical spheres, do offer a significant panorama of the difficult conditions in the Russian Church today and its attitudes towards the Western Christian traditions; this panorama is completed by N.Lossky, who writes from the perspective of the rich Russian emigrant population. The contributions by E.Lanne and A.Roccucci give the historical co-ordinates which are indispensable for providing the correct context for the problems discussed in this issue, while E.Fouilloux and A.Mellone offer critical information on the main Catholic conversation partners of the Patriarchate of Moscow: the Holy See and the 'Uniate' churches.

On the whole, despite its inevitable incompleteness, the complex picture which results from these contributions proves at the same time to be not only full of problems but also immensely fascinating. The Holy Russian Church is emerging from the trial under the Soviet regime strengthened by the fruitfulness of its faith in the quest for a cultural recovery – after seventy years of silence – in a social world which is in a tumultuous process of change, besieged by the ungenerous and short-sighted onslaught of proselytism. The quest for renewal in fidelity to its traditional identity is as fascinating as it is difficult.

Therefore we ask readers to share the desire for brotherly awareness which has inspired this issue, but at the same would suggest to them that they should not be satisfied with what we have succeeded in presenting on this occasion. The complexity, the variety and the riches of the Russian Christian tradition are enormously greater. It is important for this issue, rather than satisfying a desire for knowledge, to serve to stimulate a desire for even more knowledge.

We owe a special debt of gratitude to Cardinal F.König of Vienna, who kindly accepted an invitation to contribute an article to this issue. This is also an authoritative testimony to the commitment to begin a new stage in brotherly relations between the Roman Catholic tradition and the Russian Orthodox tradition. We owe no less a debt of gratitude to Georgy Zyablitsev of the Department for Foreign Relations of the Moscow Patriarchate, who has not only contributed to the issue but also has played a decisive part in the project and in the choice of Russian contributors.

Giuseppe Alberigo
Oscar Beozzo

The Significance of the Baptism of Rus' in the Development of Russian Culture

D.M.Shakhovskoi

The question of the significance of the Baptism of Rus' and its influence on the development of Russian culture is bound up with the study of the original sources and the origins of Russian literature. Two literary monuments above all stand out from the Russian sources, *Slovo o zakone i blagodati* (Sermon on Law and on Grace) by Metropolitan Ilarion, and *Pouchenie Vladimira Monomakha* (Instruction of Vladimir Monomakh). These works are significant for many aspects of Russian self-awareness.

There is a vast literature on the *Slovo* of Metropolitan Ilarion.[1] It can even be said that everything comes down to us from *Slovo o zakone i blagodati* rather than from under Gogol's *Overcoat*; however, strange though it may seem, only now has a complete translation finally been made.[2] In what in all probability is the first work of Russian literature, we find not only a description of the problems bound up with the spread of Christianity in Rus', but also an account of the significance of the Baptism itself. This work also fully reflects the situation in Rus' before its Baptism, the Baptism itself, and its aspects relating to mission and the bringing of peace.

It is significant that the *Slovo* disparages the pagan past. Metropolitan Ilarion underlines this with his favourite rhetorical method, repetition: 'And now we are no longer called worshippers of idols, nor do we build temples to Satan any longer, nor do we sacrifice to the demons.'[3] It is impossible to go in detail here into the question of how this pagan past is represented. It is sufficient to note that the document gives a clear and lively account of paganism. There is a description of funerals in Rus', which depicts a collective pagan orgy of a violent character which ends with the killing of a girl offered as a sacrifice.[4] Recalling this episode, attested by the Arab traveller Ahmed ibn

Faldan, Academician B.A.Rybakov emphasizes that the adoption of Christianity 'abruptly abolished the barbarian rite of common agony, human sacrifice and the ritual killings of women'.[5] In his view, it is excessive to speak of a pagan 'culture' in the full sense of the word.

Metropolitan Ilarion clearly expressed his views on what Christianity gave to Rus'. It was like a regaining of sight: 'Then we were blind, we wandered in the falsehood of idolatry.'[6] For the metropolitan Christianity had not only a religious value, emphasized by the numerous references to the gospel, but also a historical value. According to Academician D.S.Likhachev, Metropolitan Ilarion can be said to be the first Russian writer, but he could also be considered to be the first Russian historian. According to an apt comment by N.N.Rozov, 'The *Slovo* fed the chronicles and not vice versa'.[7] Thus there is all the more reason for associating both the development 'of the account of the spread of Christianity in Rus'[8] and also the first historical evaluation of this most important fact of ancient Russian history with the name of Metropolitan Ilarion. The Baptism was not only the rejection of paganism; it also made Rus' a new people, a 'people of God', and brought it the grace of God. This is the main significance of the criticism of Old Testament law which can be found in the *Slovo*. There is a critique of the Old Testament from the perspective of the gospel, but in part also from a political perspective, in that ancient Rus' wanted to distinguish itself from the Judaism of the neighbouring Khanate of the Khazars. Likhachev has seen this critique as the revelation of the basic significance of the calling of the pagans, adding that here we can also find the echo of 'direct criticisms of Byzantium'.[9] The Baptism took place, 'not in an unknown and insignificant land but in the land of Rus', which was known and famous in all four corners of the earth'. It had put its great prince, who 'had become an autocrat over his land',[10] on the same level as the apostles.

Thus justifying his glorification of St Vladimir, Metropolitan Ilarion emphasized the dignity of the prince, who not only 'wanted with all his heart to become a Christian' but, and this is even more important, 'that his land, too, should become Christian'.[11] Developing these last two points, the author emphasizes the significance of the sacrament of baptism. The description of Vladimir's baptism seems to him to be the new prototype of the salvation of humanity, the passage from darkness to light, the Easter renewal and the choice by virtue of which the divine grace passes to the people entrusted to him, diffusing itself according to the will of the prince 'over all his land'.[12]

Vladimir is called blessed for this act of spiritual heroism: 'Truly, blessedness came upon you... You, O blessed one... turned to Christ, having understood solely thanks to your good intelligence and acute intellect that there is one God... and that He sent his most beloved Son into the world for salvation. And after reflecting on this, you entered the holy baptismal font. What to others seemed foolishness, you understood as the power of God.'[13] Having emphasized that the prince did not content himself with what he heard but put what had been said into practice, showing love towards his neighbour, the metropolitan remarks: 'What a glorious salvation did you gain?' Vladimir deliberately adopted the new name of Vasily at baptism because it expressed both the idea of devotion and that of power. Here Vladimir resembled Constantine. The parallel drawn by Ilarion between the Byzantine emperor and the Russian prince in part emphasizes symphony, the accord between church and state in Byzantium: Vladimir, 'meeting frequently with our new fathers, with the bishops, consulted with them in great humility about how to establish the law among our people who had only recently come to know the Lord'. So if they are equal in everything else, Vladimir is as much worthy of 'glory and honour' as Constantine is.[14]

In this way, and with the words quoted earlier, the metropolitan canonizes the prince and proclaims him holy, inviting the people to general rejoicing. Addressing Vladimir directly and exclaiming 'Arise', Ilarion passes from the oratorical and hortatory genre to the ecclesiastical and liturgical genre, combining the forms of the *akafist* (hymn) and those of the prayer of invocation (*moleben*): 'Rejoice among the rulers, O apostle, because you have raised not dead bodies, but those who are dead in the spirit... Rejoice, our teacher, guide of faith... Pray, O blessed one, for your earth and for the people over whom you have reigned with justice, because the Lord has kept it in peace and in the faith handed down by you, and because the true faith is glorified in it, and because all heresy has been eradicated, and because the Lord God has preserved it from all warlike invasion and captivity, from famine and all pain and adversity.'[15]

This definition of holiness shows how deeply and rapidly the gospel teachings were disseminated in the minds and hearts of ancient Russian society. The martyrdom of the princes Boris and Gleb is a demonstration of this. The principate of Yaroslav the Wise pursues the symphony indicated by Ilarion. The Chronicles emphasize Yaroslav's love of books, his close relations with the clergy, his faithfulness to the church and its rules, and also his activity as an aedile.

> In the year 6545 (1037), Yaroslav founded a great city; near the city are the Golden Gates. He also founded the church of St Sophia, the metropolitan church, and later the church of the Annunciation of the Mother of God at the Golden Gates, and also the monastery of St George and St Irene. And in his reign the Christian faith began to bear

fruit and to be propagated, and the monks began to increase and the monasteries began to rise. And Yaroslav loved ecclesiastical rules, he had a great love for the priests, above all for the monks, and he applied himself to the reading of books, often reading them night and day. And he gathered many scribes who translated from Greek into the Slavonic language. And he wrote many books. The believers studied them and benefited from the divine teaching. Just as if one ploughs the earth, another sows and yet others gather and have food in abundance, so too it happened then. His father Vladimir had ploughed the land and made it fertile, i.e. ventured the Baptism. He sowed in the hearts of believers the words of books; and we are reaping, having received the teaching of the books. The usefulness of the teaching of the books is great; since the books indicate and teach the ways of penitence, and in the words of the books we find wisdom and temperance. They are like rivers which water the universe, founts of wisdom; they are therefore of an immeasurable depth; with them we comfort ourselves in sorrow; they are the reins of temperance... As we have said, Yaroslav loved books, and having written many he put them in the church of Saint Sophia which he himself had built... And he founded other churches in the cities and the villages, nominating priests and giving them stipends, ordering them to instruct the people as had been prescribed by God, and to go to church often.[16]

The last words of Yaroslav the Wise (for the edification of his sons before he died) testify to the full and profound perception of the 'grace' of which Ilarion had spoken:

Behold, my sons, I am leaving this world; love one another as if you were brothers born of the same father and the same mother. If you love one another, God will be with you, and will subject your enemies to you. And you will live in peace. But if you live in hatred, dissent and discord, then you will perish, and destroy the land of your fathers and your grandfathers, the land which they conquered with great difficulty.[17]

Christian awareness became united with state responsibility to such a degree that for a while it even manifested itself in family relations, as the marriages of the prince and his sons bear witness.

The bonds of kinship among the Russian princes of that time are considered an indication of the political and diplomatic significance of ancient Rus'. It can be added that they also bear witness to the high level of its culture.[18] Records with the signature of Anna the daughter of Yaroslav the Wise are still preserved in the French archives, while her husband

Henry I signed only with a cross. Another thing that these marriages demonstrate is no less important: Rus' was considered by the other mediaeval states of Western Europe to be one of the main Christian states. The Russian princes married into the main dynasties of that time, and the blood of Charlemagne began to run in their veins. While this did not have a particular significance for the Russian princes (it is possible that no one was even aware of it), it was a great honour for the Western houses to be related through them with the leading sovereigns of the Christian world, the Byzantine emperors.

Vladimir Monomakh represents the best example of the Christianization of Russian society from the end of the eleventh and beginning of the twelfth centuries. His work, precisely because it is that of a layman, bears witness to the penetration of Christian ideals in the development of the ancient Russian culture of that time and its continuity from Prince Vladimir, his great-grandfather, passing through Yaroslav the Wise, his grandfather, and Yaroslav's favourite last son Vsevolod, the father of Vladimir Monomakh. Despite all the impediments of this world, love for one's neighbour and pacification are the main aims of the life of this prince. The *Pouchenie* of Vladimir Monomakh is the only 'example of political and moral teaching' in ancient Russian literature, 'presented not by a churchman but by a statesman'.[19] To these words of O.V.Tvorogov it should be added that particularly from this perspective, the work of Prince Vladimir Monomakh is of exceptional interest as an expression of everyday life. We should look at the *Pouchenie*, produced in 1117, together with the *Pis'mo* (Letter) written in 1096 by Vladimir Monomakh to Prince Oleg Svyatoslavich. Forgiving the death of his son, the prince then exhorted Oleg to brotherly love, reconciliation and work for the land of Rus'. His letter confirms a state of mind with which the *Pouchenie* is pervaded; it ends with a prayer just like Metropolitan Ilarion's *Slovo o zakone i blagodati*.

If in a first examination of the *Pouchenie* our attention is likely to be focussed on the ethical conceptions of Vladimir Monomakh, on a closer examination of this literary monument its eschatological character become increasingly clear. The prince begins the *Pouc'ene*, like all his other works, with a prayer: 'Seated on my sleigh (in my declining years), I reflected in my mind and I praised God.'[20] In his message to his children he recalled the baptizer of Rus', 'in his baptism called Vasily, with the Russian name Vladimir'. In this way Monomakh emphasizes the blessing which falls on them through the grandfather, father and mother of the house of Monomakh.

The first thing that he teaches his children is faith in God, the care of salvation in their own souls. 'First of all, for love of God and for your soul, have in your heart fear of God and give abundant alms, as this is the principle of all good.'[21] Shortly before this, the reflections of the prince assume the character of a prayer, in all probability under the influence of the Psalter; it is clear from the quotations that he has also used other books. The spiritual words of his readings echo the thoughts of the prince himself, who in accordance with Holy Scripture indicates the way by which the salvation of the soul can be achieved: 'Like a father, now loving, now punishing his little son and then loving him again, so too our Lord has shown the way in which to conquer one's enemies, how to be freed from them, and how to conquer them through three good actions: penitence, tears and charity. And you, my children, do not disregard the divine commandment, so that with these three actions you can be freed from your sins and will not be deprived of the heavenly kingdom.'[22]

Prayer is the main instrument of salvation. It is important to pray at every moment, day and night. 'Do not sin even for a single night; if you can, prostrate yourself to the earth; if you do not have the strength, bow three times... And when you ride a horse, if you do not converse with anyone, if you do not know other prayers, say silently within you "Lord have mercy." Because to repeat this prayer is better than to think of futile things as you travel... After raising your morning praise to God, then, having seen the sun in its rising, you should again glorify God with joy.'[23]

According to the prince, the greatest obstacle to salvation is laziness: 'And for the love of God do not be overcome with indolence, I beg you; do not neglect these three actions. They are not laborious; it is not a matter either of being an anchorite, or of the monastic life, or of the fasting which other just men impose on themselves, but of obtaining the divine mercy in small actions.'[24] With other words the prince emphasizes that salvation is in the hands of all and does not require an asceticism beyond one's own strength (here too he mentions monasticism, as something which calls for a particular asceticism). The clergy are presented as a help: 'As for the bishops and the abbots, respect them and receive the blessing from them in love. Do not keep away from them, and as far as you have strength, love them and provide for them, and by virtue of their prayer seek to obtain the grace of God.'[25] How close Vladimir Monomakh is to the church is emphasized by the fact that the prince 'himself supervises ecclesiastical order and rites'.[26] But prayer alone is insufficient for salvation; works are also necessary: 'If you are able, do good, and if you are not able, then study, for so my father did, remaining at home and learning five languages, and thus received honour from other countries. Indolence is the mother of everything: it makes those who are capable forget, and prevents those who are not capable from learning.'[27] Following the commands of the Gospels, which he knows well, Vladimir exhorts his children to seek piety: 'Prepare, faithful one, to act out of piety, heed the word of the Gospel: "Love the one who hates you."'[28] Love is the commandment which Vladimir does not neglect, reminding Oleg, 'Whoever says "I love God but not my brother" is a liar.'[29]

If we compare the *Pis'mo* with the *Pouchenie* it is clear that the latter is a survey of a career during which Vladimir has meditated on his own affairs, on his relations with people, trying to find the way towards the kingdom of God among worldly preoccupations. His advice is not the expression of a simple ethic, but an aspiration to the kingdom of heaven. This is not always clear to a contemporary mind. The question consists in the capacity to discern, as far as possible, the depths of a distant era and the psychology of people at that time. So 'we must detach ourselves from the customary evaluations and understandings with which we approach the literary works of modern times and try to imagine as fully as possible the specific conditions in which literature developed in this or that country in the time which we are studying'.[30] In the light of these words of O.V.Tvorogov it is difficult to judge the literary monuments of ancient Russia without a religious training. This is particularly the case when these monuments prove to be corner-stones in the Russian self-understanding.

The term 'Russian self-awareness' might recall another more modest jubilee. A century ago M.O.Koyalovich, professor at the Theological Academy of St Petersburg, published the monograph *Istoriya russkogo samosoznaniya* (History of Russian Self-Awareness). Alongside the study of various monuments of ancient Russian literature, in this work there is a first attempt to establish a historiography of the Russian church.[31] By way of conclusion, one must emphasize that this work is a stock-taking of an experience lasting over a thousand years. Consequently it generalizes, and the history of Russian self-understanding cannot be separated from the history of Russian holiness, of Russian monasticism, of the Russian clergy, and also the history of Russian society.

Despite its desire to be independent, the Russian Orthodox Church has always been extremely concerned about canonical unity with Constantinople. The patriarchate in Rus' was instituted only with the consent of the other sister churches. This is also relevant to some difficult pages of our church history. It is improbable that the separation could have been achieved without the influence of the Patriarch of Antioch; the Synod was instituted with the consent of the Ecumenical Patriarch.

V.N.Tatishchev, a Russian thinker from the first half of the eighteen century, despite all his enthusiasms, wrote the work *Dukhovnaya* (Spiritual Testament), the content of which is very close to the *Pouchenie*; it can be considered a philosophical-theological reflection. The nineteenth century saw on the one hand a symbiosis of theological, philosophical and historical thought, but on the other hand the formation of parishes. It is with good reason that at the beginning of this century a poet said of the Word of God:

> We have set a limit to it,
> the wretched limits of nature,
> and like bees in a desert
> we scent the dead words.[32]

But in the last century in particular, 'in the night of speculative conceptions',[33] a fundamental question was raised again: 'Please explain to me why it is ridiculous to believe in God while it is not ridiculous to believe in humanity. Why is belief in the kingdom of heaven shocking, while to believe in an earthly utopia is intelligent?'[34] It can be presupposed that A.I.Herzen, who wrote these words, was also nurtured on the pure sugar of the Russian Orthodox Church which, as at its beginning, so too now, recalls the light of love.

Notes

1. N.N.Rozov, *Sinodal'nyj spisok sochinenii Ilariona – russkogo pisatelya XI veka* (Synodal manuscript copy of the works of Ilarion, a Russian writer of the eleventh century), 1963; L.Müller, *Des Metropoliten Ilarion Lobrede auf Vladimir den Heiligen um Glaubensbekenntnis*, 1963; id., *Die Werke des Metropoliten Ilarion*, 1971; N.N.Rozov, *K voprosu ob uchastii Ilariona v nachal'om letopisanii Letopisi I khroniki* (The question of the participation of Ilarion in the initial redaction of the Annals and the Chronicles, 1973), Moscow 1974.

2. A.M.Moldovan, *Slovo o zakone i blagodati* (Sermon on the Law and on Grace), Kiev 1984 (translation edited by Deacon Andrek Jurcenko, presented to the participants in the International Ecclesiastical Historical Conference on the Baptism, Kiev, 21–28 July 1986).

3. Ibid., 181 a.

4. A.P.Kovalecskij, *Kniga Akhmeda ibn Faldana o ego puteshestvii na Volge v 921– 922 godakh* (The Book of Achmed ibn Faldan on his Voyage on the Volga in 921–922), Char'kov 1956, 141–6; A.P.Nonosel'tsev, *Vostochnye istochniki o vostochnykh slavyan i Rusi VI–IX vekov* (The oriental sources on the Eastern Slavs and Rus', sixth to ninth centuries), in A.P.Novosel'tsev, V.T.Pasuto, L.V.Cherepnin, V.P.Susarin, I.N. Shchapov, *Drevnerusskoe gosudarstvo i ego mezhdunarodnoe znachenie* (The Ancient Russian State and its International Significance), Moscow 1965, 398.

5. B.A.Rybakov, *Yachestvo drevnikh slavyan* (The paganism of the ancient Slavs), Moscow 1981, 281–3.
6. Moldovan, *Slovo o zakone i blagodati* (n.2), 181 b.
7. Rozov, *K voprosu ob uchastii Ilariona* (n.1), 36.
8. D.S.Likhachev, *Russkie letopisi i ikh kul'turno-istoricheskoe znachenie* (The Russian Chronicles and their historical-cultural significance), Moscow and Leningrad 1947, 51–75.
9. D.S.Likhachev, *Natsional'noe samosoznanie drevnei Rusi. Ohcerki iz oblasti russkoi literatury XI–XVII vv.* (The national self-awareness of ancient Rus'. Essays on Russian literature of the eleventh to seventeenth centuries), Moscow and Leningrad 1945, 26–7.
10. Moldovan, *Slovo o zakone i blagodati* (n.2), 185a.
11. Ibid., 186a.
12. Ibid.
13. Ibid., 189a.
14. Ibid., 191a–b.
15. Ibid., 194b.
16. *Povest' vremennykh let* (Tale of Bygone Years), I, 102–3.
17. Ibid., 108.
18. N.Baumgarten, 'Généalogie et image occidentaux des Rurikides russes du X au XIII siècles', *Orientalia Christiana* 35; V.T.Pasuto, *Mezhdunarodnoe znachenie drevnei Rusi – Istoriya, kul'tura, etnografiia i fol'klor slavyanskikh narodov* (The international significance of ancient Rus'. History, culture, ethnography and folklore of the Slavonic peoples), Moscow, 47–62.
19. *Istoriya russkoj literatury*, Leningrad 1980, 59.
20. A.S.Orlov, *Vladimir Monomakh*, Moscow and Leningrad 1946, 129.
21. Ibid.
22. Ibid., 135.
23. Ibid., 139.
24. Ibid., 135.
25. Ibid., 137.
26. Ibid., 149.
27. Ibid., 139.
28. Ibid.,133.
29. Ibid., 157.
30. *Istoriya russkoj literatury* (n.21), 19.
31. M.O.Koyalovich, *Istoriya russkogo samosoznaniya po istoricheskim pamyatnikam i nauchnym sochineniyam* (The history of the Russian self-understanding according to historical monuments and scientific works), St Petersburg 1884, 510–20.
32. N.S.Gumilev, *Sobranie sochinenii* (Complete Works) II, Washington 1964, 39.
33. A.Blok, *Sobranie sochinenii* (Complete Works) III, Moscow and Leningrad 1960, 304.
34. A.I.Gerzen, *Polnoe sobranie socinenii i pisem* (Complete collection of works and letters) V, Petrograd 1917, 467.

The Three Romes

Emmanuel Lanne

From the fifteenth century, Moscow has presented itself as the Third and last Rome. In Russian eyes the first Rome was considered to have failed by reason of schism and heresy; the second, Constantinople, had fallen into the hands of the infidels in 1453, having yielded to the pressures of the old Rome in 1439. Moscow, capital of a principality which had courageously freed itself from the barbarians of Asia, could take over as the centre of the Christian world. An ideology was born. We need to note its elements. The claim to be a third Rome was recognition that the prestige of the first two Romes, namely that of the older or ancient Rome, and the younger or new Rome, had been very great. In fact for more than ten centuries Old and New Rome had been the two poles of Mediterranean Christianity. So Moscow aimed to create a new pole to supplant the first two, a pole which was shifted northwards.

From the beginnings of Christianity the prestige of the first Rome had been immense and incontrovertible. Even when the empire became a persecutor and its capital was identified with Babylon the great harlot, as in the Revelation of John (17.1), Rome remained Rome, the *Urbs*, the City *par excellence*. On being accused Paul appeals to Caesar (Acts 25.10); this brings him before the imperial tribunal in Rome. At the very moment of his arrest he had claimed the status given him by his Roman citizenship (Acts 22.25), and the centurion who had laid hands on him showed, like Paul, the utmost respect for a title which directly associated a man with the capital of the empire, its law, its institutions and its civilization.

Christian faith very soon spread outside the frontiers of this Roman empire, and yet Rome was so bound up with the origins of the gospel preaching that, for better and above all for worse, it remained one of the obligatory points of reference for any catechesis. Jesus had suffered under Pontius Pilate, the representative of Rome. The account of the passion, the nucleus of the Gospel accounts and the heart of the creed of primitive faith, attaches the mystery of Christ to human history by the name of the Roman procurator (cf. I Tim.6.13). Rome, the capital of the Empire, is thus the necessary pendant to the small country in which the sacred history and the work of salvation unfolded. First, certainly, came Judaea and Jerusalem, but then came Rome, which was indissoluble from them.

Rome, the capital of the empire, was also the place of the martyrdom of Peter and Paul, the greatest among the apostles, and of their burial. The combination of these two facts explains the unique place held by the City from the beginning. Though there is no need unduly to emphasize the importance of the chain of witness which attaches a quite special significance to the martyrdom of these two first apostles from the first century on, this chain exists and is unique in the history of Christianity.

Some links in this chain are essential. Between 96 and 98, or even earlier according to some recent authors,[1] and at any rate before the end of the composition of what was to become the New Testament, the letter of Clement of Rome bears strong witness to the significance of the martyrdom of Peter and Paul in Rome (I Clem.5.3–7). Such is the tradition which goes back to the apostolic era; it crystallized in the course of the first centuries, making the see of Rome the chief among the episcopal sees of the Christian world, by reason of the glorious testimony given there by the first two apostles. Even when the supremacy of the apostolic authority of the see of Rome was contested in the name of another apostolic authority, as already happened with Polycrates of Ephesus during the dispute over Easter towards the end of the second century, no one doubted that the church of Rome had a status beyond compare and that this status was due to the combination of the unique place of Rome, capital of the empire, and the martyrdom of Peter and Paul which had taken place there. Here we can cite the famous formula of St Irenaeus of Lyons on the origin of the church of Rome 'founded and established by the two most glorious apostles Peter and Paul'.[2] Eusebius of Caesarea, who knew the work of St Irenaeus well, constructed the whole of his *Church History* on the succession of emperors, but also on that of the bishops of Rome. While he gives lists of the bishops of Alexandria, Antioch and Jerusalem, the list of the bishops of Rome is determinative for him. This was the situation up to the Council of Nicaea and the dedication of Constantinople by Constantine in 330. And even then nothing changed in the absolute and undisputed pre-eminence of the see of Rome among the other episcopal sees of the Christian world.

From the Council of Constantinople in 381 and above all from Chalcedon, the new civil and ecclesiastical place now occupied by the New Rome, Constantinople, led to a shift in the situation. Constantinople did not seek to supplant ancient Rome; nevertheless from the beginning it encountered the categorical and almost fierce opposition of the papacy, the source of many of the later misunderstandings. Thus there arose in Rome, probably under Damasus, the theory of the three Petrine sees which made Alexandria, through St Mark, and also Antioch, dependent on the see of Rome. This theory, advanced over the centuries against Constantinople by the papacy,[3] was the great argument of Pope St Leo for rejecting the all too famous Canon 28 of the Council of Chalcedon. For St Leo, the apostles Peter and Paul played a fundamental role in connection with the church of Rome and even the city of Rome, which eclipsed that attributed by history and legend to Romulus and Remus. A fusion developed between the political idea of Rome as *caput orbis* and the Christian idea of Rome as the place of the martyrdom of Peter and Paul.[4] A sermon of St Leo's for the festival of Peter and Paul is particularly significant in this respect: Rome, 'you who were mistress of error, have become the disciple of the truth', since these two first apostles 'founded you better and with more good fortune than those who traced your first outline (Romulus and Remus), for one of these gave you your name at the cost of a fratricide'.[5] The two new founders of Rome thus attached themselves to that binary series which was of such mythical importance, but in place of the murder of one of the two by the other, it was the martyrdom of both which established it, even if here again one of the two, Peter, was to gain primacy over the other. In Leo's perspective the apostles Peter and Paul have made Rome the new capital of Christianity. Its bishop is quite simply the *episcopus plebi Dei*, bishop for all the people of God, as the triumphal arch of the basilica of Santa Maria Maggiore has solemnly announced since 435–440.

At this time New Rome had already become important, as a pendant, if not as a rival, to the first Rome. The historian Socrates, who wrote around the same time, claims that the name 'Second Rome' was the one Constantine preferred for the city that he had founded on the Bosphorus.[6] In fact Constantine did not conceive Constantinople as a second Rome, but as an extension of the first and forming one with it. 'In this unitary world of which Constantine is the symbol, there is no more room for two capitals than there is for two orthodoxies. Constantine did not found Constantinople for Rome's loss, but to give it its former glory.'[7]

Even if things had begun to change in the reign of Constans II, the first document which formally attests the name of New Rome and draws canonical consequences for its church is later. This is the famous Canon 3 of the Council of Constantinople in 381 according to which 'the bishop of Constantinople has the prerogatives of honour after the bishop of Rome, because this city is the New Rome'. With Theodosius I, in fact, Constantinople definitively took its place as capital. In 395 the division of the empire created a new context. Until then the two Romes simply made up a single capital of a single empire. From then on there were two Romes. In 421 the Theodosian Code laid down that the new capital inherited all the privileges of the old.[8]

However, for a long time old Rome was to ignore the existence of Canon 3 of the 381 Council of Constantinople, just as it was to ignore the creed produced by the same council. At the conclusion of the Council of Chalcedon in 451, however, it had to take note of the facts. Eusebius of Dorylaeum had read this Canon 3 of Constantinople before Pope Leo and the latter had not protested.[9] Now the text which was to become Canon 28 of Chalcedon had the sole aim of spelling out these prerogatives of Constantinople, New Rome.[10] 'Following the decrees of the holy Fathers in all things, and recognizing the canon of the 500 bishops,' Canon 3 of Constantinople, 'which has just been read, we take and vote on the same decisions on the matter of the prerogatives of the most holy church of Constantinople, New Rome. The Fathers rightly granted its prerogatives to the see of Old Rome because this city is the imperial city. For the same reasons the 150 very pious bishops have granted equal prerogatives to the most holy see of the New Rome, rightly judging that the city which is honoured by the presence of the emperor and the senate, and which enjoys the same prerogatives as the old imperial city of Rome, is as great as that is in ecclesiastical matters, being the second after her,' hence its supremacy over Pontus, Asia and Thrace and over the dioceses of the barbarian regions.

The legates of Pope St Leo protested and made their protest a matter of record. St Leo also protested and a serious crisis between the two Romes ensued. Pope Leo objected to the emperor Marcian 'that there is a difference between the temporal order and the ecclesiastical order, and the apostolic origin of a church, its foundation by the apostles, is what assures it an elevated rank',[11] and he spelt this out: 'Let Anatole of Constantinople content himself with being the bishop of the imperial residence, since he cannot in any way make it an apostolic see.'[12] In fact it was only later that Constantinople would claim the apostolic foundation of its episcopal see by St Andrew, and then it did so very timidly.[13] In Old Rome the opposition to the promotion of Constantinople to the second rank of the order of ecclesiastical sees lasted beyond St Leo to Popes Gelasius and Symmachus. It was not until the reign of the emperor Justinian (527–565) that the order of the five sees of what would be called the 'pentarchy' was officially recognized, Old Rome clearly occupying first place. In fact

Justinian rediscovered the spirit of Constantine and considered the two Romes, Old and New, as ideally making a single city, the centre of the world. This is the spirit in which we have to understand Novella CXXXI: 'Following the decisions of the councils we decree that the most holy pope of Old Rome is the first of all the hierarchs and that the holy archbishop of Constantinople – the New Rome – occupies the second see, after the holy and apostolic see of Rome but with precedence over all the other sees.'

After Justinian and above all in the course of the seventh and eighth centuries, relations between the two Romes deteriorated on both the political and the religious levels. The ideological break came about only with the creation of the Frankish empire. The coronation of Charlemagne by the pope at Christmas 800 is the symbol of this break. The iconoclastic crisis was another contributory factor. Now the two Romes no longer followed a common course. When the Photian crisis arose, a break developed between the two churches which has left traces down to our day, even after the re-establishment of relations and the rehabilitation of the Patriarch Photius. With the agreement made in Canon I of the Council of Saint Sophia in 879–880, the two Romes recognized their canonical independence from each other, but relations between them remained difficult. In 1054, the papal legate Humbert de Moyenmoutiers excommunicated Michael Cerularius, the patriarch of Constantinople, without having the authority to do so, and the latter acted likewise towards Old Rome. This canonical and sacramental rupture was more symbolic than real, but it clearly shows how alien the two sees had become from one another.

However, the Byzantine emperor needed the West because of the increasingly strong pressure on the Turks after the defeat at Manzikert in 1071. From then on the relationship between the two Romes was even more than before to develop at two levels: that of religious relations between the two churches, and that of political relations between the pope, head of Western Christianity, and the Byzantine emperor. There would be constant interference between these two registers, but in the end, up to the fall of Constantinople in 1453, it was the relationship between the pope and the emperor that would prove decisive.

However, in 1204 there was a catastrophe – the capture of Constantinople by the Crusaders – which created an irreparable breach between the two churches and the two parts of Christianity. The fall in 1453 is already implied in that of 1204. The two and a half centuries which separate the two events are those of the agony of the second Rome, to which the first Rome made an effective contribution.

The Third Rome, Moscow, was born out of the political fall of the second Rome. So the historical context is different from the one which had given rise to Constantinople as an extension of ancient Rome. The ideology of Moscow as the Third Rome has its roots in Bulgaria during the last brilliant period of the reign of John Alexander in the middle of the fourteenth century.[14] He had already been given the title of 'Orthodox Tsar by the Grace of Christ the Lord and Autocrat of all the Bulgars and Greeks', and a eulogy on this same tsar, composed in 1337, already contains the ideology of a Third Rome: not Moscow, however, but Trnovo. However, as F.Dvornik once remarked, the Byzantine political ideas passed into Kievan Rus' much earlier, namely already with Vladimir. But it was with Andrei Bogolyubsky, Prince of Suzdal and Vladimir (died 1175), that they reached their peak.[15] The conjunction of the Bulgar ideology and that of Kievan Rus' could have played a part. Maximus, a Greek, became Metropolitan in 1283. In 1299–1300, keeping the title of Kiev and all Rus', he established his permanent residence at Vladimir on the Klyazma river in northern Russia.[16] The devastations of the Tatars had made it impossible for him to stay in Kiev. He died in Vladimir in 1305.

From 1308, his successor Peter, Metropolitan of Kiev, resided permanently in Moscow while retaining jurisdiction over Kiev and Vladimir. In fact he had two dioceses, Kiev and Vladimir, and controlled the capitals of the two Russias, Moscow and Vilna. He had permanent vicars at Kiev, Vilna and Moscow. The departure of the metropolitan for the north momentarily prompted the creation of a metropolitanate in Galicia and in Lithuania. The Orthodox of these regions in fact were defenceless in the face of the proselytizing imperialism of the West. However, the authority of Moscow was considerably reinforced by the transfer of the metropolitan see of Kiev from Vladimir to Moscow in 1326, and then with the great figure of Metropolitan Aleksi (1354–1378). One of his successors, his contemporary Metropolitan Kiprian, was Bulgarian by origin and a friend of the Greeks. He was sent as apocrisarius to Moscow in 1370, and then consecrated Metropolitan of Kiev in 1375, with the right of succession to Vladimir-Moscow (1390–1406). Five years later, in 1380, the Muscovite victory of Kulikovo took place, which was to mark the end of Tatar hegemony.

Up to that point, however, the vast metropolitan area of Kiev-Vladimir-Moscow had no intention of competing with the second Rome, on which it continued to depend canonically. The change took place only with the Council of Florence (1438–1439). The Metropolitan of Kiev and all Russia, Isidor, a Greek, was one of the promoters of union with the Latins. The Grand Prince Vasily II of Moscow rejected the union and had Isidor thrown in prison. He managed to escape and never returned to Moscow. Vasily's successor, Ivan III, who succeeded in annexing most of the neighbouring principalities to Muscovy, had had Iona elected as Metropolitan of Moscow in 1448. Iona no longer commemorated the patriarch of Constantinople, who from then on was considered schismatic and heretical for having accepted the union of Florence. In 1453 Constantinople fell into the hands of the Turks. Ivan II took as a second wife Zoe Sophia Palaeologus (1472), niece of the last emperor of Constantinople, and adopted Byzantine ideas on imperial autocracy. It is true that Ivan III never claimed the *translatio imperii* from Constantinople to Moscow, but it has to be recognized that the whole context favoured the birth of the new ideology which made Moscow the Third Rome. The successor to Metropolitan Iona, Feodosy, was elected 'Metropolitan of Rus'' and no longer bore the title of Kiev; this marked the independence of the see from Constantinople.[17]

This ideology of Moscow as the Third Rome was explicitly formulated only at the beginning of the sixteenth century by the monk Filofei of Pskov in his famous letter to Grand Prince Vasily III, successor of Ivan III: 'The first Rome was destroyed because of its heresies, the second Rome fell victim to the Turks. The first and second Rome have failed, but the third will last to the end of history, for the last Rome, Moscow, will have no successor. A fourth Rome is inconceivable.'[18]

A new stage was completed under Ivan the Terrible, when in 1547 he assumed the title Tsar, Caesar, the old imperial Roman title. Finally, under Boris Godunov, in 1589, the patriarchate of Moscow was created by Jeremiah II, Patriarch of Constantinople. He only acted because of the pressure put on him by Boris Godunov. He wanted Jeremiah II not to return to Constantinople but to establish himself in Moscow.[19] The rescript which established Iov as patriarch of Moscow quotes almost literally the famous letter of Filofei: 'The old Rome failed because of the Apollinarian heresy. The second Rome, Constantinople, is under the yoke of the sons of Hagar, the impious Turks. Your great Russian empire, O pious sovereign, the third Rome, surpasses them in piety and all the pious kingdoms are united in yours. You alone under heaven will be called Christian Tsar throughout the world by all Christians.' The new patriarch titled himself 'Iov, Patriarch of Moscow, city of the Tsar, and of all Russia, the new Rome'.[20]

With Peter the Great the ideology of Moscow as the Third Rome seemed to disappear. The new emperor moved the capital to St Petersburg and abolished the Moscow patriarchate in 1721. The 'white klobuk', the headdress reserved for the patriarch, the legendary symbol of a Roman succession, was given to all the metropolitans. However, despite this concern for secularization, we know that at the end of this same century Potemkin dreamed of recapturing Constantinople from the Turks and establishing the grandson of Catherine II there as emperor.

The last avatar of Moscow as the Third Rome is more of a paradoxical metamorphosis: this is the myth put forward by V.Soloviev in *Russia and the Universal Church* (1889), in which 'Romanism' in its many often contradictory senses is under the surface everywhere with the famous play on words, *Roma-Amor*.

Since then Moscow, the third Rome, having again become the capital of Russia, has practised a seesaw policy towards the Second Rome, disputing its primacy among the other Orthodox churches and eventually establishing direct relations with the First Rome. From the beginning the Moscow patriarchate sent observers to the Second Vatican Council, whereas the other Orthodox churches did not attend (some, like Greece and Romania, would never send any observers). When at the end of Vatican II the hope was expressed of beginning a dialogue between the Catholic Church and the whole of the Orthodox Church, Moscow took the initiative in opening a direct dialogue with Rome. To the present day the three Romes remain, each in its particular role, the main conversation partners in the dialogue between the Christian communions.

Notes

1. Cf. Joseph Ysebaert, *Die Amtsterminologie im Neuen Testament und in der alten Kirche. Eine lexikographische Untersuchung*, Breda 1994, 211.
2. *Adversus haereses* III, 3,2. Cf. E. Lanne, 'L'Église de Rome "a gloriosissimis duobus apostolis Petri et Pauli Romae fundatae et constitutae Ecclesiae"', *Irénikon* 49, 1976, 275–322.
3. Cf. M.Maccarrone, *Apostolato, episcopato e primato di Pietro. Ricerche e testimonianze dal II al V secolo* (= *Lateranum* XLII, 1976,2), Rome 1976, 170; C.Pietri, *Roma Christiana, Recherches sur l'Église de Rome, son organisation, sa politique, son idéologie de Miltiade à Sixte III (311–440)*, Rome 1976, Vol.1, 870.
4. K.Schatz, *La primauté du pape. Son historie des origines à nos jours*, Paris 1992, 59.
5. Sermon LXXXII (LXXX),PL 54, 422 C–D. Cf. Schatz , *Primauté* (n.4), 55–9.
6. *Church History* I,16, PG 67, 116c.
7. Gilbert Dagron, *Naissance d'une capitale, Constantinople et ses institutions de 330 à 451*, Bibliotheque Byzantines Études 7, Paris 1974, 24–5.
8. C.Th.XVI, 2, 45, 14 July 421.
9. Mansi, 7, 449A.
10. Cf. A.de Halleux, 'Le vingt-huitième canon de Chalcédoine', *Studia Patristica* XIX, Louvain 1989, 28–36.

11. Leo, *Epistle* CIV, 3, PL 54, 995.
12. Ibid.
13. F.Dvornik, *The Idea of Apostolicity in Byzantium and the Legend of the Apostle Andrew*, Cambridge, Mass. 1958, 154ff.
14. Cf. M.de Taube, 'À propos de "Moscou Troisième Rome"', *Russie et chrétienté* 3–4, 1948, 23–4.
15. F.Dvornik, 'Byzantine Political Ideas in Kievian Russia', *Dumbarton Oaks Papers* 9–10, 1956, 73–121.
16. J.Meyendorff, *Byzantium and the Rise of Russia. A Study of Byzantino-Russian Relations in the Fourteenth Century*, Cambridge 1981, 79.
17. Cf. ibid., 274–5.
18. V.Malinin, *The Starets Philotheus of the Monastery of Eleazar and his Letters. A Historical and Literary Study* (in Russian), reprinted with an English introduction by H.Schaeder 1971, In the introduction Schaeder corrects and complements certain points of his basic work *Moskau das Dritte Rom. Studien zur Geschichte der politischen Theorien in der slavischen Welt*, Hamburg 1929, Darmstadt ²1957. For the quotation see ibid., Appendix, 45, and Schaeder, *Moskau das Dritte Rom*, 55.
19. Oscar Halecki, *From Florence to Brest*, Rome 1958, 229–30.
20. Schaeder, *Moskau das Dritte Rom* (n.18), 92. Cf also N.Zernov, *Moscow, The Third Rome*, London 1937, 49.

I · The Faith in Russia

The Primacy of Monastic Spirituality

Vladimir Kotelnikov

The most powerful impulse in Russian religious life comes from the monasteries. Monasticism in its best aspects and richest gifts was a reality which conveyed the spirit; the monastery and the cell of the *starets* became centres of a refined inner asceticism which led from the 'struggle against the passions' to prayer 'of the heart' and 'of the mind', the Jesus prayer. It was in the monasteries that Orthodox personalism, the necessary complement to conciliarity (*sobornost'*) in the Eastern Church, was developed.

The Christian is eucharistically bound to the whole body of the church and lives in it, but at the same time also seeks other forms of communion with God: in imitating the humility of Christ, in the awareness of his own sin, in mystical contemplation and in the ecstasy of prayer. All these are forms of the creative presence of the person before God: in them there is an element of spiritual boldness, of risk. With meekness, with obedience to the will of the Father and to his own spiritual father (*starets*, plural *startsy*), the monk discovers a higher Christian freedom, a full *parrhesia*, and enters into possession of gifts of the Holy Spirit which enrich the church and the lay culture which is close to it.

Apart from the most ancient monasteries, in which Greek monks lived together with Russian monks (for example at the Monastery of the Saviour near Vyshgorod, or the Monastery of Wisdom at Kiev), from the foundation of the monastery of the Caves of Kiev in 1062 to the time of the monasteries at Optina Pustyn, and of the Caves of Pskov, the Russian monasteries followed that synthesis of Christian gnosis and Christian practice under the sign of which the whole Eastern ascetic tradition was built up. Thus the 'royal way' was traced towards the transfiguration of human created nature, towards deification. At the heights of sanctity, the depth of understanding of spiritual realities is always united with an abundance of love and the intensity of ascetic discipline.

Russian asceticism developed in the wake of the patristic tradition. The building up of monastic life in its various forms – coenobitic, eremitical and anchoretic (hermits and recluses) – was always determined by the ancient rules (of St Saba, of Theodore Studita, of Athos), which were almost unchanged until the nineteenth century. The intimate spiritual life of the monk and the guidance of the spiritual father (the 'nutrition') were orientated on contemplative and mystical experience in accordance with the ascetical anthropology of the Holy Fathers and Doctors of the church, among whom in Russia Isaac the Syrian, John Climacus, Mark the Ascetic, Dorotheos of Gaza, Maximus the Confessor, John Chrysostom, Thalassius and Simeon the New Theologian enjoyed particular authority.

And in the 'golden century' of Russian spirituality (fourteenth-fifteenth centuries), as in the later period of the development of monasticism (eighteenth-nineteenth centuries), and in the present situation, the movement towards perfection was thought of (and practised) as asceticism on a spiritual ladder.

The ladder indicates a gradation of values and spiritual states, in that God is certainly in them all, but not in all in the same way. A ladder is a series of steps, and represents a hierarchy. In this organizing principle of reality, Christian thought very quickly expresses its own understanding of the earthly and heavenly order. In the Areopagite corpus (introduced into Russia in the fourteenth century by Metropolitan Kiprian and widely diffused in a large number of manuscripts), this principle takes on a universal character, justifying itself on a theological and metaphysical level.

The monk knows that man – in that he is called to submission to God – is himself structured in a hierarchical way and is not in fact a harmony, as the humanism of modern times wishes to persuade us. The harmony is between man and God; harmony is what is shaped in God's name. The God-man is hierarchical. There was no harmony in Eden, nor will there be harmony in the kingdom of heaven. Harmony is enclosed within the confines of the created world, with which it will end, and therefore it appears tragically beautiful and attractive. By contrast hierarchy, penetrating this world, conquers its finitude and goes beyond its limits.

The contemporary secularized consciousness continues to defend the thesis of the equal value and truth of all impulses and intentions of the 'natural man', the thesis of the legitimacy of an unlimited freedom for each individual within a harmonic whole. But this inevitably leads to an axiological relativism, from which there follows the break-up of all wholes (in the person and in society), the transformation of harmony into chaos, which today is reaching ever more disturbing dimensions.

Asceticism indicates a hierarchy of 'degrees of vision' (in the consciousness) and 'degrees of action'. Basing himself on Isaiah (11.2–3), Nicetas Stethatos, the closest disciple of Simeon the New Theologian, established seven levels, corresponding to the seven gifts of the Holy Spirit.

The first level is 'the spirit of the fear of God'. Nicetas Stethatos then differentiates between psycho-physical awareness and the spiritual vision. The true monk notes here not the sceptre of God the Judge nor the 'right hand which punishes', but the blessedness of the fear of the Lord. He can already say with Anthony the Great, 'Now I love God to such a degree that I no longer fear'.

In the monk, the fear of God means having a wakeful spirit, a ready understanding, and a will to work, all fixed on God; this is a radical theocentrism in the formation of the whole person. Blessedness consists in the fact that the fear of the Lord frees one from the fear of the created. It is no longer one's destiny to depend on the power of nature, the source of sin and death; rather, here there is a direct and free submission to the will of God, the source of grace and eternal life. The fear of God puts a limit to the existential anguish which fills the body and the spirit and which is only partly silenced by cultural anaesthesia.

The nearer the monk gets to the top of the spiritual ladder, the more complete the transfiguration of human nature becomes: the passions cease to act in a destructive way (this is the substance of ascetic impassibility); the consciousness arrives at contemplation, that super-consciousness which, as it loses its former content, becomes apophatic unconsciousness. Ascending to divinization, the human reason, in the words of Maximus the Confessor, proves to be a 'little logos' which reflects in itself the great Logos, while the soul achieves the state of absolute peace.

At that moment, says Isaac the Syrian, the 'inner man' reveals itself 'by the activity of the spirit corresponding to that rank it will have in immortal and incorruptible life; because as it already takes part in this [world] *in mysterio* in a resurrection of the mind, it is a true testimony to universal resurrection'.[1]

Isaac the Syrian was thinking here not of mental contemplation of the resurrection but of a real arrival by human beings at a new state above the natural state. This is certainly an acquisition which is not yet wholly definitive or total, but it is real, at least to the degree that human beings accept the grace of God.

The necessary condition for progressing on the ladder is humility. To be humble means to direct all one's being on the way of the will of God, conquering two obstacles which are almost insurmountable for the 'outer man': love of self and self-will, which interpose themselves on the way of our love towards God and the neighbour. A courageous mind and firm moral resolve are therefore necessary; true humility is far from being easy for all to practise.

Humility as an ethical and religious ideal very quickly became rooted in Christian Rus', and in a lasting way. The figures of the first Russian saints, Boris and Gleb, remind us of this. The influence of this ideal is evident in the individual consciousness and the national ethos: it is there in the birth of the nation as such. Here we often find a kenotic humiliation which reaches the extreme limit indicated by Isaac the Syrian: to humble oneself 'is to make oneself nothing, almost non-existent, not yet come to being'.[2]

The Russians also were also to adopt this peculiar 'absence of being' in other ages. This does not mean that they went outside the world-historical process; but there are certain moments in which participation in this process ceased to be the positive primary task for them. Spiritual energy concentrated at other points, where the problems of faith and conscience are decided; at that time the themes of suffering, sacrifice and penitence took on special significance. Among the expressions of this type of tendency are the calls to self-limitation in the private, political and technocratic sphere made today by A.Solzhenitsyn, V.Belov and V.Rasputin.

However, here it is inevitable that the most external pole of human activity gives way to the elemental principles of nature, to the interplay of constructive and destructive forces in which the Russian easily becomes involved, even at the risk of his own happiness. It is then that we find the dark Russians, full of heroism, abnegation and foolishness for Christ's sake (*yurodstvo*). But to organize is to give shape to one's own existence in accord with the laws of natural reason and sensual beauty, constantly to move, in a systematic way, to a stable systematization in the world; all this takes hard work to bring about, and is rarely crowned with success. The important thing is to withdraw humbly from all this, to resume one's existential nakedness, in the unshakeable persuasion that this is not shameful, because it is confirmed before God by love for Christ who humbled himself to the death of the cross.[3]

The culmination of monastic prayer is the Jesus prayer. The Lord is not only invoked but present in this act of communication with Him. This is attested by the experience both of the ancient monks and of the ascetics of our time like Fr John of Kronstadt and some monks of the onomadox (Name-Glorifying) movement.[4]

The Eastern tradition knows three models of Jesus prayer. Oral prayer is offered in constant remembrance of the Lord and by the effort of the will, intent on repeating the formula of the prayer many thousands of times a day until the person who is praying succeeds in remaining in absolute inner purity and gentleness. At this level the Jesus prayer is work, asceticism, effort. The second model is mental prayer: the mind concentrates on the name of Jesus and feels nearness to the Lord without being distracted by anything, enclosed in the 'inner rest' of hesychia. The third model is the prayer of the heart: the mind descends to the heart and then the prayer rises incessantly without any effort of the will. Now Jesus himself, present in the invocation of his name, leads the one who prays to deification, leading the spirit to the ecstatic contemplation of the light of Tabor, the divine operations of the Logos.

Gregory Palamas provided a speculative foundation for the possibility of contemplating the uncreated light of the Transfiguration, developing the notion of the substantial unity and at the same time of the difference between God and the operations and energies which proceed from God. These latter, while belonging to the unattainable substance of God, differ by being attainable by and accessible to spiritual contemplation, to which those who practise the 'prayer of the heart' are elevated. The Palamite doctrine (a truly hesychastic theology) has proved to fit particularly well with the spiritual and mystical intuitions of the Russian ascetics, from the fourteenth century to our day. Over these centuries, monasticism has sought to preserve the continuity of this 'prayer of the mind and heart', handing down this 'science of sciences' from spiritual father to disciple, from expert to beginner.

A number of extraordinary monuments of spiritual literature which describe the mystical and religious quest of the ascetics in prayer have emerged from the monasteries. One of these texts is widely known (and not only in Russia) and has been published many times. This is the *Sincere Talks of a Pilgrim to his Spiritual Father*.[5] Three principle themes are evident in the book: the unquenchable thirst for a true knowledge of God which arises in the person who lives out an ascetic enthusiasm in the world; a profound humility, which arises out of the awareness of one's own weaknesses and one's own sins; and finally the spiritual feast and the luminous joy of mystical insights. The penitential and confessional tone of the *Accounts* is set alongside passages which derive from the Fathers and have a strictly doctrinal character; it is evident that the author of the book is a monk involved in the ministry of the *starets*, who has gone through all the levels of the spiritual ladder, but who is also a master of the style of literary composition.

Another less known manuscript is the *Notes on the Experiences of Life* by Arseny Troepolsky. It is probable that some copies were in circulation among the monks and in circles close to the monks, and this has led to variations in the published versions.[6] A lyrical-intimate tone is dominant in Troepolsky's account of his condition of prayer; he goes through all its aspects in a perceptive and very fine way, from spiritual enthusiasm to physiological sensations. In his finesse and sincerity of expression he is very close to the tradition of Christian poetry, in particular that associated with the name of Ephraem of Syria and Gregory of Nazianzus.

However, this type of literature is far from exhausting the inner experience of monasticism. Sometimes the monk may leave no literary trace, as happens in the case of Serafim of Sarov. Monastic spirituality, which runs through all of Christian Rus' in a lively and uninterrupted stream, is realized above all in ascetic practice. And here the most important figure is the *starets*.

There are situations (which every believer knows) in which a person is not in a position by himself to take on the 'legacy of the Spirit', to free his own will from the prison of the world, to return to himself and to God within him. Human beings find themselves in a sorry state of being closed to Christ, in the situation of Lazarus, already covered by a tombstone, when only a little ray of spiritual light remains as a pledge of the resurrection of the dead.

Then, to conquer this closedness, spiritual communication is needed with a *starets* who knows how to guide towards God, with a monk who is an expert in 'inner activity'.

What happens then? A spiritual communion arises between the two, like the new spiritual being of which the apostle Paul speaks: Christ has destroyed the wall of separation which stood between the two, 'to create in himself, from the two, one new man, making peace and by reconciling all and both with one God in a single body, by means of the cross' (Eph.2.15–16).

To become the spiritual son of a *starets* it is necessary to perform a very difficult asceticism, that of 'breaking the will'; in other words, renouncing one's own will, following one's own desires which arise from our carnal nature. One's own personal will must become solely the will of the *starets*, in things great and small. It is not easy to achieve this. And those who do not achieve it feel not only the weight of obedience and the pain of breaking with their own egocentric nature but also a feeling never known before, of freedom from all that seemed a precious treasure of the 'I' and which were in reality only carnal excrescences on the spirit. Konstantin Leontyev, who had passed the hard test of killing the will in practice, and not just in books, having become a spiritual son of Amvrosy of Optina, related:

> Do you not know, for example, what sweetness there is in consigning all one's own knowledge, one's own culture, one's own vanity, one's own

proud susceptibility, into the hands of a *starets* who is simple, but expert and honest? What Christian will is necessary to kill in oneself the other will, the will of the world?[7]

Another irrevocable law of obedience to the *starets* is 'openness of thoughts', the continuous and absolutely sincere confession of all the movements of the soul, waking and sleeping. The will of the *starets* is directed to Christ; those who follow the *starets* follow Christ, as Simeon the New Theologian incessantly emphasized. He has left the tremendous image of the luminous chain which binds to the source of all light, with an incessant 'outpouring of light' through the celestial hierarchy and a picture of the saints who ascend to it, each united with the last saint closest to him (in order of time). Spiritual union with the *starets* makes us a link in the 'golden chain' which leads to uncreated light.

The *starets* is a guide of the spirit to God; he restores to his spiritual son the divine sonship which the son has lost. With this, the union with God through the *starets* in no way runs contrary to ecclesial and liturgical communion (something of which sometimes the *starchestvo* [the practice or institution of *startsy*] is accused without reason). In the same way, 'opening the thoughts' to the *starets* does not supplant the sacrament of confession and does not break the secrecy of the confessional. G.P.Fedotov has given a precise definition of *starchestvo*: it is 'an institution which makes a bridge between the gifts of the spirit and service to the world',[8] and for this reason it can be considered an indispensable organ to the body of Christ, the church. For many people down to the present day, a relationship with a *starets* very often becomes the only way of conquering their own condition of orphanage with respect to God. Basil the Great had seen the monastery as a little church; in the same way the *starets* with his own spiritual sons forms a little church, like the disciples with their master at the head.

The *starets* is certainly also the source of a love which can warm, guard and care for a man. The *startsy* dry human tears, support those in need, and help with counsels for life: all this is an inseparable and important part of *starchestvo*. But the *starets* reaches to an incomparably greater depth than the level of a person's creaturely needs and interests; the *starets* touched on the intimate depth of the man something that obliged him to stand absolutely alone before God, to recognize keenly his own personal fault before God, and to discern his own personal way of salvation.

In *starchestvo*, the principle of conciliarity (*sobornost'*) typical of the Eastern tradition is united with the element of Orthodox personalism. In dialogue with the *starets* we free ourselves from all that is not personal in us or is part of a false personality, and save ourselves from being dispersed in the world. The *starets* in fact always and solely speaks to the inner self; he does good and loves my own self in depth, brings me together, who am scattered on all sides, and opens my whole being to Christ.

The authentic obedience experienced with a *starets*, with a full 'killing of the will' , with the 'disclosure of thoughts', is the encounter of the two persons in Christ – without confusion and without division, to use trinitarian terminology. It is not a belittling of the person but the growth of the person to the stature of the God-man, in reciprocal submission and the openness of love.

These are the contents which made and still make monastic spirituality the heart of Christianity. Different circumstances in the history of the church can have obscured it, but they have not changed its fundamental role.

Among Russian ascetics, saints and anchorites there have always been some exceptional figures, who have been able to bring a new spiritual energy to monasticism, to the religious life. After Feodosy of Pecersk, the most important figure of this type was Sergei of Radonezh.

With him the monasteries did not have great changes in order (with the exception of the introduction of the coenobitic rule in many monasteries) or in regular discipline, but they were deepened in a significant way and the asceticism of the Spirit was intensified, and mystical and contemplative tendencies were reinforced. This was the period of the renewal of links with Athos, of increased interest in the patristic writings on asceticism and above all the spiritual experience of hesychasm. The introduction of the reading of the *Synodikon* of Orthodoxy, with the fifteen new articles that were inserted in the fourteenth cenutry, the first six of which expound the fundamental theological and metaphysical thesis of hesychasm, contributed to the spread of this last. But the destiny of these ideas is characteristic: they did not in fact become the object of theoretical disquisitions, and the echoes of the Palamite controversies were quite weak in Russia, even if their content was well known. Hesychasm became an instrument of 'inner activity', of monastic practice. Certainly, in monasticism this led to the development of a particular kind of 'mystic individualism', though this never reached the extremes of what Leontyev called 'transcendental egoism'. Both Sergei himself and those who pursued his work (Kirill Belozersky, Dionisy Glusitsy, Ioasaf Kamensky and then Nil Sorsky and others down to Serafim of Sarov and the *startsy* of Optina) were able to harmonize this form of spirituality with concrete love of the neighbour and charitable activity in the world.

What emerges at the first level in the work of Nil Sorsky is the discipline of the Spirit, with which in time is even associated a foretaste of spiritualistic rationalism. At the summit of the work of the ascetic Nil puts moderation, tact, and like Anthony the Great he prizes in the monk the 'gift of discernment', which is the 'beacon of the soul'. He conceives of the whole course of 'inner formation' of the person as being order in hierarchy, marked by an equilibrium between ecstasy in prayer, 'sobriety of the mind' and manual labour, along with a lack of any possessions.

Russian asceticism today still bears the stamp of the personality of Nil Sorsky, the first 'intellectual saint' of Rus', according to the striking definition by Ivan Kologrivov.

From the second half of the sixteenth century onwards this current suddenly weakened; 'ritual', which is far from always keeping an authentic Christian spirituality in depth, came to dominate piety. In the eighteenth century the person came to be increasingly dominated on the one hand by the frenetic construction of social and state structures from a diverse secular culture, and on the other was put under too severe supervision by the synodical authorities. This did not stop an inner decline, both in the monasteries and outside.

However, gradually, in the ecclesiastical monastic sphere, opposition began to arise to such a tendency. This led to the 'silent reform' of Russian spiritual life, characterized by a return to the sources of Christian spirituality. It was initiated by Paisy Velichkovsky. In quest of the 'revelation of man' from an authoritative master, Velichkovsky left Russia and, after staying in some *skity* in Wallachia *(skit* = cell, hermitage; *skity* = communities of monks), established himself on Athos. Thanks to his enormous energy, numerous patristic works were rescued from oblivion (the majority of which were found in the library of the monastery of Vatopedi), translated and then published. The translation of the *Dobrotolyubie* (*Philokalia*) of Paisy marked the beginning of the renaissance of Greek patristics in Russia and the re-establishment of the Christian tradition in its integrity. Having himself becomes an authoritative *starets* on Mount Athos, Paisy consolidated the *starchestvo* in the monasteries of Dragomirna and Neamts, and later, through his very numerous disciples, in the Russian monasteries.

A real triumph of monastic spirituality is represented by the *startsy* of Optina Pustyn, the direct heirs of Paisy. The three great *startsy* of Optina represent the three phases of the struggle and rebirth of the human spirit. In Fr Leonid we clearly find the voluntaristic beginning of asceticism, a feat (*podvig*) of ascetic labour. For some he recalls Jacob in the Old Testament, when in the sweat of his brow he worked for Laban, first to obtain Leah and then Rachel. In Makary there appears the spirit which raises itself above the bodily nature, conquering the 'demons of the soul'. He was given Leah, but the marriage with Rachel would have required a way of new trials and hard asceticism. The spirit triumphs with Fr Amvrosy; fully possessed by the human nature the spirit rests on it; the *starets* therefore walked – it seemed – without touching ground (or at least that was the impression of those who knew him). Amvrosy was immediately given Rachel, who was soon to give birth to Joseph.

Their contemporaries wrote at length on the *startsy* of Optina, and recently so have various scholars. So I would refer the reader to the relevant sources,[9] and will limit myself here in conclusion to sketching out the general outlines of the movement.

Something happened at Optina similar to what happened in Christianity after the fourth century: the encounter of holiness with the world, the task of the gospel with history, ascetic discipline of the Spirit with the psychological elements of the human being.

The cultural landscape created by the ascetics of Optina, the natural and architectural aspect of the monastery, are stamped with the features of the spiritual style of the hermit. Before us we have the substance of the world transfigured by prayer and love: the luminous faces of the monks and their slight figures moulded by prayer and love (we might remember Nesterov's picture), the abundant fruits of the earth, the smile of the woods; the churches, the *skity*, the walls marked with love and prayer. This is the style of eschatological optimism, in so far as it is still possible to express it in psycho-physical forms, to incarnate it in a material which is still earthly. It is not possible to stylize such a model or to imitate it; it arises out of the Spirit, by grace.

Optina recalls urgently that Christianity is not a 'period' of universal history which has now finished or nearly finished, but a divine-human process which still goes on, which leads us all to the transfiguration of human nature: 'We shall not all sleep, but we shall all be changed, in a moment, in the twinkling of an eye' (I Cor.15.51–52). Optina reminds us that the seed of God is not dead in us, but lives in one person in secret, while in another it is clearly germinating and promises much fruit.

Certainly civilization has followed and is following its course, in accordance with the historical level of providence: the first act of creative liberty performed in Eden has still to have its ultimate consequences. Anthopolatry will still triumph for a long time, and through the cultural chatter of the 'outer man' will silence the voice of the 'inner man' (as these are distinguished in Paul, Rom.7.22 and II Cor.3.16).

Nevertheless, in the depths of the soul, men recall where the true source of life is. Not all recognize it fully, and those who decide to put it into practice are even fewer, but each person feels that Babylon – whether of the Old or the New Testament – is not a construction remote from life and that the road leads to other horizons; sometimes we feel their call very clearly.

It is possible that the development of monastic spirituality means that the world, in its present state of the 'confusion which precedes death' (K.Leontyev), is entering into a new phase of relationship with the Christ Logos and is approaching the threshold of a qualitative new Christian influence. Perhaps we have not entirely lost the capacity for this model of the Christian organization of society and culture which we know from the period of the high Middle Ages.

Notes

1. *Ascetical Writings*, 28.
2. *Dobrotolyubie* II, Moscow 1895, 681.
3. This topic is developed in T.Goriceva, Yu Mamleev, *Novyi grad Kitezh (Filosofskii analiz russkogo bytiya)*, Paris 1989.
4. The problem of the Name-Glorifiers goes back to the time of the controversy over the name of God from 1912–1913, which was occasioned by a book by the schimo-monk Ilarion, *Na gorakh Kavkaza* (On the Mountains of the Caucasus). The book appeared in 1908 and was then reprinted many times. The polemic attracted the attention of many Russian theologians and philosophers: Archbishop Feofan (Bystrov), Bishop Feodor (Pozdeevsky), Father Pavel Florensky, M.D.Muratov, M.A.Novoselov, S.N.Bulgakov, V.F.Ern and others. See also the priest-schimo-monk Antony Bulatovich, *Apologiya very vo Imya Bozhee i vo Imya Iisusa*, Moscow 1913; S.N.Bulgakov, *Filosofiya imeni*, Paris 1953 (French translation, *Philosophie du verbe et du nom*, Lausanne 1991); A.F.Losev, 'Filosofiya imeni', in id., *Iz rannikh proizvedenii*, Moscow 1990; R.Salizzoni, *L'idea russa di estetica. Sofia e Cosmo nell'arte e nella filosofia*, Turin 1992, 147–89.
5. The most complete edition was published in Paris in 1989, with an essay by the hieromonk of the monastery of Simono Petra Vasilij (Grolimund) on Athos. See also S.Bol'sakov, *Na vysotakh dukha. Deyateli molitvy Iisusovoi v monastyryakh i v miru (Lichnye vospominaniya i vstrechi)*, Brussels 1971.
6. There is a lithograph copy of the manuscript in the archive of Optina Pustyn (*Otdel rukopiseij Rossiiskoi gosudarstvennoi biblioteki*, F.214, no.411). I have quoted some passages of this manuscript in V.Kotel'nikov, 'Pravoslavnaya asketika i russkaya literatura', *Prizma* 15, St Petersburg 1994, 28–30.
7. K.N.Leontyev, *Otshel'nichestvo, monastyr' i mir. Ikh sushchnost' i vzaimnaya svyaz' (Chetyre pis'm s Afona)*, Sergiev Posad 1913, 13.
8. G.Fedotov, *Svyatye drevnei Rusi (10–17 stoletiya)*, Paris ³1985, 235–6.
9. Here I shall list only a few: I.L., *Skazanie o zhizni i podvigakh blazhennoi pamyati startsa Optinoi pustyni ieromonakha Makariya*, Moscow 1861; *Zhizneopisanie optinskogo startsa ieromonakha Leonida (v skhime L'va)*, Moscow 1876; Archpriest S.Chetverikov, *Zhizneopisanie optinskogo startsa ieroskhimonakh*

Amvrosiya, Kozel'skaya Vvedenskaya Pustyn', 1912; S.A.Nilus, *Na beregu Bozhei reki*, Troitso-Sergiev Posad 1916 (reprinted California 1969); V.Lossky, 'Les *starets*i d'Optino', *Contacts* 13, 1961, 4–14; id., 'Le *starets* Léonide', *Contacts* 14, 1962, 9–19; id., 'Le *starets* Ambroise', *Contacts* 14, 1962, 219–36; I.Konysevich, *Optina pustyn' i ee vremya*, Jordanville, New York 1970; V.Kotel'nikov, 'Optina Pustyn' i russkaya literatura', *Russkaya literatura* 1, 3, 4, 1989; *Il santo starec Amvrosij del monastero russo di Optina,* edited by the monks of the Russian Uspenski monastery of Rome, Abbazia di Praglia 1993 (with a large bibliography)

The Theological Conceptions of the Slavophiles

Aleksi I. Osipov

Among the Russian Orthodox thinkers, the so-called 'lay theologians', none have left so deep a mark on the theology of the Russian church, in particular on its ecclesiology, as the first Slavophiles. However, in our church circles, in the theological schools and even among professional theologians, none are so little known as they are. Paradoxical though it might seem, the names of philosophers like V.S.Solovyev, who openly defended Spinoza's pantheism, fervently admired the idea of the primacy of the pope and defined the Orthodox Church as 'the 'Greco-Russian Synagogue';[1] N.A.Berdyaev, who took no account of the holy tradition of the church and proclaimed the 'primacy of freedom over being'; N.F.Fedorov, a pseudo-scientific writer who exhorted everyone to 'the common enterprise', or to 'make the fathers rise again'; or V.V.Rozanov, with his open insults against Christ and the church are more familiar. So too are those of other thinkers, Russian or not, often far from the church and Christianity. But what about the names of the Slavophiles: A.S.Khomyakov, I.V.Kireevsky, K.S. and I.S.Aksakov, Yu.F.Samarin, A.I.Koselev and others? Yet they were profound and sincerely Orthodox thinkers, who were able to found an original religious and philosophical system, zealous to the point of sacrifice and heroism in the guardianship and development of an independent original, national autochthonous culture.

Why are these Slavophiles so little known? That is a question which is too complex for us to be able to resolve here. I shall limit myself to making some essential points. The Russian 'society' of their time (not the people!) was so far from the church, and the official theology taught in the schools was so impregnated with scholasticism that the struggle of the Slavophiles for the formation of their own Russian culture, for a return to the experience, now discredited, of the knowledge of God characteristic of the

Church Fathers, inevitably appeared equally alien to both the former and the latter. 'Society' saw the appeals of the Slavophiles to national character (*narodnost'*), to Orthodoxy, to knowledge in the unity of love, as a kind of obscurantism.[2] For official theology, the references to the theological thought of the Fathers inevitably seemed a threat to...Orthodoxy![3] For precisely this reason, A.S.Khomyakov, the recognized head of the Slavophiles, did not see his theological works published in Russia. They appeared for the first time only in 1879, nineteen years after his death. The fate of his companions' works was in many respects similar. Here too it is possible to see one of the reasons for Slavophiles' lack of 'popularity'. The one major expert in the work of Khomyakov before the Revolution, Professor V.Zavitnevich, rightly wrote:

> Even now, Khomyakov still remains largely unknown to us. Khomyakov is not recognized because he is not understood; he is not understood because he is not studied; and he is not studied because the conditions in the life of the educated class in our society, both intellectual and even more religious and moral, were not and are not sufficient to favour the study and the understanding of this great figure. Still baptized with the restrictive name Slavophile, even today he wanders through our society with that wretched label which hides him from the eyes of people who read little and have even less idea of the marvellous riches and variety of the real content of the mind of this man of uncommon gifts.[4]

So far, the theological, philosophical and literary gifts of the Slavophiles have not been much investigated. Nevertheless, a century after the age in which they lived, the Slavophiles still maintain their significance. Thus the problem of 'Russia and the West' continues to appear on the agenda today, perhaps with even greater urgency, whether in the social and cultural sphere, the theological sphere, or in those areas in which the contribution of the Slavophiles was so great.

What new contribution did the Slavophiles make to Russian theology? In connection with the answer to this question the well-known adage 'the new is the old that has been well and truly forgotten' *(vse novoe – eto khorosho zabytoe staroe)* immediately comes to mind. This applies very much to the work of the Slavophiles. If the essence and specific character of their theological conceptions (and not just those) had to be expressed in one word, that word would be ecclesiality *(tserkovnost')*. In all their theological works we see the most sincere attempt to express some truth of the faith on the foundation of the holy tradition of the church, of the synodical understanding which this produced, and not according to 'the elements of this world', the passion of philosophical reason or schemes fixed by the theology of the schools, essentially scholastic and Western in spirit, in form and often in ideas.[5] The criterion of ecclesiality is the one basic criterion which the Slavophiles used with full awareness throughout their literary and practical activity, primarily in theology. And it is not just the case that the basic theme of their works was the problem of the One, Holy, Catholic *(Sobornaya)* and Apostolic Church. For them this was not an abstract or theoretical problem but a vital one. In their eyes, a failure to understand it had made a solution to all the substantial problems of thought, culture and history impossible.

The interest of the Slavophiles was concentrated above all on identifying the causes and nature of those processes in the religious and cultural life of the West which had made Russia so profoundly different. Thus they were deeply persuaded that the main cause was that new and radically false conception of the church which had been developed at the end of the first millennium in the Church of Rome and had become normative throughout the West. This reading of the doctrine of the church also led to a corresponding development throughout the life of the Western peoples. As Khomyakov wrote, 'the division of East and West on the religious level has a significance for people's lives throughout European history'.[6] So it was necessary to clarify the essence of Orthodoxy and how it differed from the two basic directions followed by Western Christianity, Catholicism and Protestantism. This also explains the generally polemical character of the theological treatises of the Slavophiles, primarily those of Khomyakov, who most of all wrote on the church.

For him, the question of the church was the starting point and at the same time the final result of all theological research. Fr P.Florensky, speaking of the significance of Khomyakov for Slavophilism, rightly comments:

> Three-quarters of any question about the Slavophiles amounts to a question about Khomyakov, and the group of Slavophiles itself thought of itself as 'Khomyakov and the others'... Khomyakov was and remains the ideal centre and head of Slavophile thought not only, or better not so much, *per se* but also by virtue of the position which he occupied. He was in fact the main seeker for that holy centre from which the thoughts of the Slavophiles are drawn and to which they return: Orthodoxy, or more precisely, the Church... Slavophilism is a vision of the world expressly connected directly with the Church, and Khomyakov is the centre of the group of Slavophiles, the undisputed

authority of Slavophile thought... Khomyakov's thought is wholly about the Church.[7]

These are very true words, even if Florensky is not always objective in his judgments on Khomyakov. But Khomyakov is in fact the main theologian among the Slavophiles: he produced by far the majority of their theological writings; and in them the main space is taken up by reflections on the church.

The problem of the church is a vast and complex theme, above all in the specific form that it assumes in Khomyakov. For him the church is not one of the realities of Christianity but the nucleus, the nub, of all the factors which determine human life in all its extent, in all its dimensions: religious and social, spiritual and material, individual and collective. It is truly the 'leaven' of all human life.

So what is its nature? What personality is to be found in it? What happened to the church in the West and how has Christianity been understood in Roman Catholicism? What consequences did the schism have for Western Christianity, for the moral and social life of the West and for its philosophical thought? And finally, on what basis is it possible to re-establish the unity of Christians of East and West, and with them the foundation of an integral culture?

These are some of the questions which form part of the general theological system of the Slavophiles and which we shall see taken up in the exposition which follows.

Among Khomyakov's works is one entitled *Attempt at a Catechetical Exposition of the Doctrine of the Church* (*Opyt katekhizicheskogo izlozheniya ucheniya o Tserkvi*) or, as he himself renamed it, *The Church is One* (*Tserkov' odna*). This work and the three very short writings entitled *Some Words of an Orthodox Christian on the Western Confessions* (*Neskol'ko slov pravoslavnogo khristianina o zapadnykh veroispovedaniyakh*), together with the letters to Palmer,[8] constitute the main sources for the study of Khomyakov's theological works.

The Church is One begins with a definition of the church (an unusual definition and therefore all the more significant for understanding Khomyakov's whole system):

[The] unity [of the Church] follows of necessity from the unity of God; for the Church is not a multitude of persons in their separate individuality, but a unity of the grace of God, living in a multitude of rational creatures, submitting themselves willingly to grace... The unity of the Church is not imaginary or allegorical, but a true and substantial unity, such as is the unity of the many members in a living body.

The most notable thing about this definition is in the first place the decisive emphasis on the divine humanity of the church, the unity through participation in God of all creatures who welcome the divine grace. Secondly, there is the decisive negation of the anthropocentric character of the church understood as a society, or a totality of persons 'in their separate individuality', who have the same faith, the same baptism, one head of the church, etc. (an idea which had become common in the theological courses in the schools,[9] and which put the church alongside the parties, associations, organizations of a purely human character). In this way the church, according to Khomyakov, is not a community of persons bound together by identical conceptions, a rule or a cult; no, all this is not the church, because such community and unity can also be found in other religions, and in Christian communities separated from the Orthodox Church, or those who belong only outwardly to the church (cf. Rev. 3.14–19). For Khomyakov, the church is the unity of many members in the living Body of Christ, to which it is possible to belong through the work of the Holy Spirit. 'The visible Church,' he writes, 'is not the visible society of Christians, but the Spirit of God and the grace of the Sacraments living in in this society.'

What is the main basis of the inner life of the church? What is the sign that makes it possible to judge that this is the church? Khomyakov replies:

> This is the principle of conquering love in Jesus Christ, which bears its fruits in itself: sanctification and knowledge of the divine sacraments, or, to put it another way, faith. The visible Church also exists in order that such a principle may subsist and be recognized by all, even in the absence of a widespread awareness of the external aspect. But when the very principle is denied, then what was the visible Church ceases to exist in the real sense (44).
>
> This is the rule of the visible Church; it subsists only to the degree that it subjects itself to the invisible Church, and consents to put itself at the service of the manifestation of this. On the other hand the invisible Church, by its very nature, evidently cannot recognize as its manifestation a so-called society which does not intend to submit itself to the very principle of the Christian communion (191).

Khomyakov sets this understanding of the church over against the reductive conception which, in his view, arises and finds expression in the West in concrete forms.

There is a substantive difference between the idea of the Church which considers itself a unitary organization, whose living principle is the divine grace of reciprocal love, and the idea of Western societies, whose unity, thoroughly conventional, consists for Protestants in the simple arithmetical sum of a given number of individuals who have gathered around the same aspirations and the same faith, and for the Romans only in the coherence of the movements of subjects of a semi-spiritual state (109).

In polemic with exponents of Western Christianity, above all Catholics, Khomyakov emphasizes in particular the basic fact that Christ,

did not entrust the custody of the faith and the transmission of his teaching to individuals, His disciples, but to the Church of the disciples, freely united by the holy power of mutual love, and it is this earthly Church, and not the persons which constitute it for the moment, that will be glorified on the day of Pentecost by the gifts of the Spirit of God. Every confession of faith, every teaching handed down, also receives its sanction, or more precisely the testimony to its truth, from this Church and by this Church and from and by it alone' (134).

One of the most characteristic features of the ecclesiological doctrine of the Slavophiles is the idea that the church is the witness to the truth and not an external authority. In his first article on the Western denominations Khomyakov had written:

'The Church is an authority', said Guizot in one of his most important works; and one of his critics, reporting these words, confirmed this; because neither the one nor the other have any falsehood and they contain no blasphemy... No, the Church is not an authority as God is an authority, as Christ is an authority; because for us authority is something exterior. It is not, I say, an authority but truth, and at the same time the life of the Christian, his inner life, because God, Christ, the Church live in him a more real life of the heart than that which beats in the breast, more real than the blood which flows in the veins; but they live in him to the degree to which he himself lives out the universal life of love and unity, namely the life of the church (67).

This idea of Khomyakov's is developed in one of the letters of K.Aksakov:

In the sphere of faith there is no authority, and authority does not bring the freedom of the spirit. For me Christ himself is not an authority, because for me He is the Truth. Note that Christ said to his disciples, 'Unless you are in me, the Spirit of Truth will not be in you' (cf. John 16.7). I understand that as follows: you believe in Me as a Head, as an authority, and not as in the Truth. That is also how I explain the famous temptation of Isaac of the Caves. Christ came to him in glory with the angels and said to him, 'Isaac, dance!' How could he not obey Christ? Isaac began to dance and became dumb and blind. It was a temptation. Where was Isaac at fault? (Certainly!) he obeyed Christ. But he was at fault because he had looked to Christ as to a Head, to an authority, and not as to the Truth. He obeyed, but behaving as someone who behaves on earth as to a commander, without discernment, and he rejected freedom. Had he examined himself, had he looked to Christ as to the Truth, he would not have fallen into error and would then have seen that this was not Christ, but that under the aspect of a Sovereign, a Tsar, he was being tempted by the spirit of lies, and tempted with blind dedication to his own head, with a foolish readiness to carry out his command... Hence it was a sin, a lie.'[10]

The very idea of the question whether the church is an authority or the Truth did not arise casually among the Slavophiles, but derived from the criticism of the idea of the primacy of the head of the church of Rome, which they were convinced had made the Roman Catholic doctrine of the church profoundly deviant. Khomyakov wrote:

> The authority of the pope, who has occupied a place of ecumenical infallibility, was an external authority. A Christian, once a member of the Church, once a participant and responsible for his decisions, was made a subject of the Church. The two ceased to be one: the Christian found himself outside the Church, while remaining within it. The gift of infallibility, attributed to the pope, was established independently of any type of connection with moral presuppositions, so that neither the corruption of all Christendom nor the personal corruption of the pope itself could have any effect on this infallibility. The pope was made a kind of oracle, deprived of any kind of freedom, a kind of flesh and bone idol (66).

With their vigorous polemic against the authoritarian and external authority of the church, which they considered, according to the word of the Apostle, to be the pillar and foundation of the truth (I Tim. 3.15), the Slavophiles at the same time sought to bring out what was essential within the church, what made the Christian who participated in it a real member, not a nominal one. Khomyakov wrote:

External unity is the unity manifested in the communion of Sacraments; while internal unity is unity of spirit. Many (as for instance some of the martyrs) have been saved without being made partakers of so much as one of the Sacraments of the Church (not even Baptism) but no one is saved without partaking of the inward holiness of the Church, of her faith, hope and love; for it is not works which save, but faith. And faith, that is to say, true and living faith, is not twofold, but single (44).

For Khomyakov, the 'moral law of mutual love' is the sole foundation of an organic totality and the law of being of the church (119). He emphasizes that 'the Church does not consist in the more or less significant number of the faithful, but in the spiritual bond which unites them' (186). It was the internal, spiritual aspect of the church and of man which above all attracted the attention of the Slavophiles: 'The Church is not an Academy,' Khomyakov commented; 'it embraces all the inner man and aims at making the mystery manifest in the world for the glory of God. The most important thing in man is not the feeling, or the knowledge, but the work, or the baptismal confession, of Christ.'[11]

This confession of Christ is faith. Certainly, Khomyakov rightly comments that

> faith is a principle by its very moral nature; but it is a moral principle which does not include in itself the tension to make itself manifest; with that it would show its impotence, or better its annihilation, its non-being. The manifestation of faith is also a work, since it is true that the stammering of prayer, hardly conceived in the depth of a desolate heart, is itself a work like martyrdom. The difference between the two lies only in the time and the circumstances in which it pleases God to fill man with the gifts of grace (118).

Christian faith is not rational adherence to a determinate number of truths, called dogmas or confessions. Such a confession is a purely intellectual fact, and therefore does not reveal God to man.

> Rough and limited reason, accepted by the passions of a perverted will, does not see God, nor will it ever see God. It is extraneous to God like evil, to which it is subject. Its belief is no more than a logical speculation and can never become faith, even if it often wants to claim such a name. Belief transforms itself into faith and becomes an inner movement towards God himself only through holiness, through the grace of the Spirit, the giver of life, the source of holiness (172).

He writes elsewhere:

Faith is not belief, nor a logical conviction based on deductions, but much more. It is not an act of one faculty of the conscience isolated from the others... Faith is not just mere thought or mere feeling, but so to speak comes both thought and felt; in a word, it is not just knowledge, but knowledge and life (73).

Only a free moral choice through Christ bears witness to the truthfulness of the faith of the Christian and of his membership of the church. Nothing can force a person to this choice. Nothing and no one, not even God himself. 'The Saviour,' Khomyakov writes, 'removed his visible presence from sinners, yet the Church rejoices.' Why does it rejoice? Because 'the visible Christ would have been so to speak an imposed, irresistible truth (through the material perceptibility of his manifestation), but it pleases God for the truth to be acquired freely. The visible Christ would have been an external truth, and it pleases God that it should become internal for us through grace in the gift of the Spirit of God. This is the meaning of Pentecost' (194).

'The Church,' writes Samarin, 'welcomes only free persons into its bosom. Those who offer a servile recognition, without believing in it, are not in the Church or of the Church.'[12]

Unfortunately the West, according to Khomyakov, has lost that understanding of freedom which the church announces and offers, falling into disastrous extremisms. These extremisms found blatant expression among the Roman Catholics and the Protestants. For the former 'the Church consists in a single person, the pope' (78). For the latter it consisted in a multitude of persons who thought differently or in the same way. However, both destroy the church: the former do away with personal freedom in the name of external unity, while the latter dissolve the unity of the church in the name of personal freedom. In both cases the result is not conciliarity (*sobornost'*) or the organic totality of the church.

'An external unity,' Khomyakov states, 'which denies freedom and is therefore insubstantial: that is Roman Catholicism. An external freedom which does not provide unity and therefore is equally insubstantial: that is the Reformation...' (198).

But 'the Church cannot be a harmony of discordant voices; it is not the arithmetical sum of Orthodox, Latins and Protestants. The Church is nothing unless the fully inner harmony of faith is matched with the accord of its external manifestations (regardless of the differences between local rites' (279). 'Freedom and unity are the two forces to which the mystery of human freedom in Christ, which is our moral nature, has been entrusted, which has saved and redeemed creation through the full union between Himself and the created' (205).

Again, the unity of the church 'is none other than the accord of personal freedoms (198); ...more precisely the unity was freedom itself in the harmonious expression of its inner accord. When this living unity was rejected (viz., by Rome) the freedom of the church had to be sacrificed to obtain an artificial and arbitrary union (81). But we profess the one free Church' (109).

Khomyakov always wants to demonstrate that the church is an organism and not a mechanism, that it is a living body formed of a vast multitude of cells which are consubstantial one with another; not by an external juxtaposition of elements of similar substance, but put harmoniously together. In this idea Khomyakov, like all those who thought as he did, found the solution to one of the most important social and theological problems: that of the freedom of the person in society. This is his reasoning:

> In the Church man does not find something extraneous to himself. He finds himself here; not, however, himself in the impotence of his spiritual solitude but in the power of his authentic spiritual union with his brothers, with his Saviour. He rediscovers himself there in his fulfilment, or, more precisely, he finds that in himself there is a task... But in what way, it will be asked, can the union of Christians give to each what none has separately? Certainly the grain of salt does not receive new being from the mass into which it has been thrown at home: and that is man in Protestantism. The brick cemented into the wall does not move and progress from the place established for it in the framework of the bricklayer: and that is man in Catholicism. But every particle of matter assimilated by a living body becomes an inseparable part of the organism and itself receives a new sense and a new life: that is man in the Church, in the Body of Christ, whose organic foundation is love. Clearly the people of the West can neither understand nor take part in it, since they do not abjure the schism which is its negation; in fact the Latins think of a unity of the Church in which there is no trace of Christian freedom, while the Protestants argue for a freedom in which the unity of the Church literally disappears (108–9).

In this way, both the real being of the church and the normality of social life are equally impossible both under the 'infallible' absolutism of the authority of a single individual in which visible unity consists and even more so under the arbitrary absolutism of the opinions of individuals, which give the illusion of freedom.

> But where is unity without a supreme authority? Where is freedom without rebellion? Both can be found in the ancient, uninterrupted, unchanged Tradition of the Church. There is unity, invested with a power much greater than the despotism of the Vatican, since it is based on the power of reciprocal love. There is a freedom far deeper than the anarchy of Protestantism, because it is directed by the peace of reciprocal love. There is the refuge and the bulwark! (293).

The Slavophiles saw in the 'peace of mutual love' the condition and the supreme criterion of the authenticity of that unity and freedom enjoyed by the members of the church within it, which constitute the irreducible foundations of any organism which has life. The Christian in the church is not a slave, subjected to the authority of God, of Christ, of the council, the pope, the bishop, nor is he an anarchist who puts his own 'I', his own judgment, above all, and sees truth itself simply as one of many opinions. No, he is a free son of the Father, who forms the one Body of Christ in peace and love of his brethren.

This moral criterion indicates the reason for the great schism and all the dogmatic deviations of the Western confessions. Khomyakov does not doubt that the distancing of Rome from the Church of the East was made possible by its 'spirit of local pride' (65), by its scorn of its Eastern brothers, and by the conciliar decisions of the universal church. Khomyakov asks himself 'in what the Western schism, or to put it more precisely, the Western heresy against the dogma of the unity of the church, essentially consists' (97). He replies:

> The Western schism is the arbitrary distancing of the whole of the West, the monopolization of divine inspiration; in a word, a moral fratricide. This is the significance of the great heresy against the Universal Church – a heresy which has removed the moral foundation from faith, thus making it impossible (93).

It is in fact

> the particularistic or personal opinion, or the opinion from a particular area (it does not matter which) that within the Church has appropriated to itself the right to resolve a dogmatic question autonomously, that contains in itself the germ of the legitimation of Protestantism, or of freedom for research, removing it from the living tradition of unity based on mutual love. And so Latinism in its very rise has proved to be Protestantism... The power to decide dogmatic questions has as it were unexpectedly shifted. At one time it was the prerogative of the whole

universal church; now it has been appropriated by a particular church (65).

In this way the Roman schism, by destroying the very essence of the church, which is moral union in mutual love in Christ, in the first place made faith impossible, now leaving space only for a 'belief'; secondly, generated Protestantism; and thirdly, threatened the very possibility of a correct acquisition of the divine truth,. All this led gradually to the secularization of Christianity in the West and to the progressive development of rationalism in all spheres of life.

By renouncing its moral foundation, faith descends to the level of rationalism. At the very moment at which it tears itself apart, tomorrow, if not today, it will succumb under its blows. This is the inevitable consequence of having denied its own principles. In this formula is contained the whole history of religion in the West. Its beginning is Roman Protestantism; its sequel is German Protestantism (207).

He writes elsewhere:

I have said that the infallibility of dogma or the knowledge of truth has as its foundation in the church 'the holiness of mutual love in Christ', and that with this doctrine the very possibility of rationalism is removed, since rational clarity is made to depend on the moral law. By damaging this link, the Western schism has enthroned rationalism and Protestant indifference (103).

In Khomyakov's thought, this rationalism is destined to lead society to an inevitable conclusion: to complete incredulity and atheism. Khomyakov asserts:

The definitive triumph of scepticism in religious matters has not yet begun; but even in the present it is possible to argue, in connection with the whole of Western Europe, that now there is no longer any type of religion in it, though it is not in a position to note this (130–1).

Khomyakov again emphasizes the primacy of love, its basic significance for all aspects of the life of the church and society. It is precisely the absence of love which leads to every possible kind of anomaly, the principle of which is the destruction of the human cognitive faculty which has therefore distorted the truth. The Slavophiles develop a gnoseological conception, at the centre of which stands the doctrine of love as the necessary source and condition of any kind of true knowledge. And in fact for what reason did the schism happen? Because 'the logical principle of knowledge, expressed in the formula of the Creed, has been detached from the moral principle of love, expressed in the unanimity of the Church' (98). 'Rome has destroyed every bond between the consciousness and the inner perfection of the spirit... [while] the infallibility of dogma, and therefore the knowledge of the truth, has as its foundation in the church the holiness of reciprocal love in Christ' (68).

There is nothing unusual in the thoughts reported here, given the message of the New Testament: 'Blessed are the pure in heart, for they shall see God' (Matt.5.8), says the Lord. 'Beloved,' exclaims the apostle John, 'love one another, for love is of God and whoever loves is born of God and knows God. He who does not love has not known God, for God is love' (I John 4.7–8). The apostle Paul expressly says: 'If anyone believes he knows something, he does not know anything as he needs to know. But whoever loves God, knowledge will be given him by God' (I Cor.8.2–3). This idea of the royal significance of love in the cognitive process also permeates the whole of the holy tradition of the Church. Therefore what Khomyakov recalls when he formulates the basic law of knowledge is not a new truth but an ancient truth which has been profoundly forgotten: 'the knowledge of the divine truth is given by the reciprocal love of Christians and has no other tutor within this love...' (143). The truth does not reveal itself 'autonomously' to the individual Christian, nor to society, nor to the genius, nor to the force of reason, nor to the fullness of knowledge, but to reciprocal love, that is, to the Holy, Catholic (*Sobornaya*) Church: that is what Khomyakov means to say here.

This mutual love of Christians is not possible without the acquisition of the perfection of the Spirit in which the mind, the feelings and the desires become one, and the soul arrives at its integration *(tsel'nost')*. I.V.Kireevsky above all emphasizes this aspect, affirming that for the Christian

> there is no speculation separate from the recollection of the inner fullness of the mind, the memory of this central point of self-awareness in which resides the authentic place of the supreme truth and where there is not only the alienated reason but all the fullness (*sovokupnost'*) of the mental and psychical faculties to provide the one common sign of authenticity for the concept that reason represents, just as on the mountains of Athos each monastery has only one part of that seal which, formed by all the individual parts in the general synod of the abbots, constitutes the one canonical seal of Athos.[13]

Therefore it is 'in the very method of theological and philosophical thought' that Kireevsky sees the substantial difference beween East and West.

> In fact, by tending to the truth of speculation, the Eastern thinkers are occupied above all with the right internal condition of the spirit which is reflecting, whereas Western thinkers are more interested in the external nexus between the ideas. In order to reach the fullness of truth, the Eastern thinkers seek the inner integration (*tsel'nost'*) of reasons, or, so to speak, that concentration of the mental faculties in which all the individual activities of the spirit flow into an superior living unity. By contrast, the Westerners argue that it is also possible to reach the full truth separately through the different faculties of the soul, which act autonomously in their isolated sphere. They think of one particular sentiment as moral, another as aesthetic; the useful in its turn is thought of as a specific concept; the true is thought of with a separated judgment; and no faculty knows how things are with the other until this latter finishes its activity. We note that every way will have led to the ultimate end before all the ways meet in a single integral movement.[14]

The Slavophiles were profoundly convinced that this separation of the cognitive faculties from the mind in which the isolated logical faculty is recognized as the 'sole organ for thinking the truth'[15] lies at the origin of the error of all Western truth, both theological and philosophical. 'Reason alone, cut off from holiness, would be blind, like matter itself,' wrote Khomyakov (79). Holiness is in fact the 'integral view of the mind'.[16] It is the love which unites all the faculties of the man in a single whole and testifies that the mind has become the dwelling place of the Holy Spirit (cf. Rom.5.5). The unity of this Spirit in a multitude of rational beings is the church, to which all knowledge and all truth has been revealed. This is the basic gnoseological idea of the Slavophiles in relation to the church.

This Slavophile doctrine of the church also explains with sufficient clarity the ideas of the Slavophiles on a theme like the unity of the church.

Khomyakov, arguing that the separation of Rome from the universal church did not happen because of any particular error but because of pride, which led Rome to commit a grave act against the church, putting itself above the universal church and changing the symbol of faith, also sees the main obstacle to the re-establishment of unity in this spiritual and moral sphere.

> I am persuaded of the correctness of the view that the most important obstacle to reunification lies not in the differences, which immediately spring to view, and therefore not in the formal aspect of doctrines (as

theologians usually argue), but in the spirit which is dominant in the Western churches, in their passions, their customs and their prejudices, in that sentiment of pride which does not allow them to recognize the errors of the past.[17]

Therefore Khomyakov makes an appeal to the Christians of the West to 'perform a great practical ascetical feat (*podvig*): to detach themselves from rationalism, to repeal the excommunication pronounced against their brothers in the East, to annul all the successive decisions derived from that violation of the law, to re-establish in their own soul the unity of the church... and themselves in its unity' (94). 'To condemn the crime perpetrated by the error of your fathers against innocent brothers: that is the only condition which could restore the truth of God and save all your spiritual life from inescapable decomposition' (147).

'But indeed,' Khomyakov exclaims, 'it is so difficult to perform a pure and simple act of justice! To recognize that to have knowledge you must confess your fault before the brothers whom you have offended and say to them: "Brothers, we have sinned against you, but welcome us again, as beloved brothers." To recognize this duty and perform it: is it indeed so difficult, so impossible?' (147).

Khomyakov sees the depth of this abyss which has arisen in the course of centuries of divisions between the Christians of the East and the West, and at the same time firmly believes that the truth of God will triumph and that the insuppressible feeling of truth which is in man will be victorious over error. 'God, at a time determined by Him, will again bring all the peoples of Europe into the bosom of the Church' (207). And with these shining words of hope we think it possible also to end this article.

Here we have touched only on the smallest part of the problems (above all the central question of the church) which we find throughout the theological work of the Slavophiles. In this same area, we have concentrated almost exclusively on the ideas of Khomyakov. However, his doctrine of the church is fundamental to the theology of the Slavophiles, and is the key to the understanding of all the other theological problems raised by Khomyakov and by the other Slavophiles of the first generation. The study of their legacy is a welcome duty for the theologians of our time.

Notes

1. V.S.Solov'ev, *Pis'ma* I, St Petersburg 1908, 223.
2. K.Aksakov, recalling the social climate in which the Slavophiles first made their

appearance, writes: 'I recall... the violent burst of ridicule and insult which hailed the first words of Slavophilism' (in *Russkoe obozrenie*, 1897, 148).

3. A.S.Khomyakov, *Sobr.Soch. Bogoslovskie i tserkovno-publitsisticheskie stat'i*, izd.Zoikin, 7 (further references in the text are to this edition).

4. V.S.Zavitnevich, *A.S.Khomyakov* II, Kiev 1913, 2.

5. Fr Georgy (Flororovsky) reports the following opinion of Archbishop Anthony (Khrapovitsky) on our academic theology: 'The system of Orthodox theology is in some areas still unknown and for this reason there is a need to study the sources accurately and not to copy a system of heretical doctrines, as we have been doing for two hundred years now' (Protoierei Georgy Florovsky, *Puti russkogo bogosloviya*, Paris 1981, 482).

6. Khomyakov, *Sobr.Soch. Bogoslovskie i tserkovno-publitsisticheskie stat'i* (n.3), 285.

7. P.Florensky, *Okolo Khomyakova*, Sergiev Posad 1916, 12.

8. William Palmer (died 1879), Anglican Archdeacon and Vice President of Magdalen College, Oxford. His life's work was the reunification of the Anglican Church with the Eastern Orthodox Church. His book *Short Poems and Hymns*, dedicated to Khomyakov, was the occasion for their correspondence. The quotation below and that on p.37 are from *A Classic of Russian Orthodoxy: The Church is One*, by Alexy Stepanovich Komiakov with an Introductory Essay on Khomiakov, his life, times and theology by Nicolas Zernov. Translation by William Palmer slightly modernized by Basil Minchin, The Fellowship of St Alban and St Sergius, London 1968.

9. Cf. for example the definition of the Great Catechism (*Postrannyij katekhizis*): 'The Church is a society established by God of men united to the Orthodox faith, by the law of God, the hierarchy and the sacraments' (article 9 of the Symbol of Faith); or Metropolitan Makarij: 'The Church is a society of believers according to the Orthodox faith and of those baptized in Jesus Christ...' (*Pravoslavno-dogmaticheskoe bogoslovie* II, St Petersburg 1985, 283): 'The Church of Christ is a society of those who believe in Christ, established by the Lord, united by the Word of God, the sacraments and the hierarchy, under the guidance of the Holy Spirit for eternal salvation' (*Pravoslavno-dogmaticeskoe bogoslovie*, third ed., Part II, Saint Petersburg 1882, 211); or of Platon, Metropolitan of Moscow: 'It is an assembly of persons believing in Jesus Christ and is called Church' (Platon, mitropolit Moskovsky, *Polnoe sobranie sochinenii* I, Saint Petersburg nd, 723).

10. K.S.Aksakov, *Polnoe sobranie sochinenii* IV, Moscow 1884, 172.

11. A.S.Khomyakov, *Polnoe sobranie sochinenii* VIII, Moscow 1897, 129.

12. Yu.F.Samarin, *Sochineniyja* VI, Moscow 1887, 349.

13. I.V.Kireevsky, *Izbrannye stat'i*, Moscow 1984, 262.

14. Ibid., 221–2.

15. Ibid., 260.

16. Ibid.

17. A.S.Khomyakov, *Polnoe sobranie sochnenii* II, 324.

The Experience of the Russian Orthodox Church during the Soviet Regime

Adriano Roccucci

Between 1917 and 1991 Russian Orthodoxy found itself several times at the heart of decisive events of this century. If the basic condition of the Russian church in the Soviet period was that of a church oppressed by a regime which programmatically pursued the aim of eliminating it, its history has nevertheless been that of a complex and unforeseeable journey.

A reconstruction of the vicissitudes of Orthodoxy in the countries of the Soviet Union has often been marked by a simplified reading. The policy of persecution by the atheistic Communist state on the one hand and a church which was at times a martyr church and at others a church of collaborators have made up the main elements of a scenario which for the most part has been depicted without any shading. The historiographical debate has often been reduced to polemic, by markedly ideological studies, about the responsibility of a church accused of being prone to dishonourable compromises with the persecuting state and betraying the witness of the martyrs. Interpretative approaches have alternated, at times full of accusations and at others apologetic and justificatory, but always at the expense of a deep understanding of a laborious and complex history.

In reality the Russian church faced a unique attack, in terms of the number of victims, the duration and quality of the oppression and the type of aggression on the part of a state which aimed to take its place. The very high number of martyrs, the suffering of whole generations of Christians faced with dramatic choices in situations of unspeakable oppression, and the transmission of the faith and canonical structures to the new generations, form a kind of moral justification for the Soviet experience of the Russian church. This experience has dark and difficult pages which need to be understood in a historical perspective. This is not the place for a detailed reconstruction of the 'Soviet' journey of the Russian church; this article in fact sets out above all to identify some moments and facts which are crucial for understanding this story.[1]

The Revolution

1917, the year of the revolutions, was also a year of great significance for the Russian church, which caused a deep break in its history.[2] With Tsarist Russia there in fact ended a model of state Orthodoxy inherited from Constantine which was inspired not so much formally by the Byzantine doctrine of the symphony between state and church as by the deformed version of the submission of the church to the state represented by the synodical system introduced by Peter I.[3] When the Orthodox Tsar abdicated and autocratic power ceased to exist, the church was deprived of its head and its infrastructures. It also found itself orphaned of that conceptual system within which it had so far thought and which was based on the sacralization of the Orthodox monarch, whom the church anointed with holy chrism at the moment of the coronation.

The decree of the separation of the church from the state promulgated by the Bolshevik government at the beginning of 1918, which among other things deprived the church of its status as a person in law, brought about a rift in the union between state and national church which had been a constant in Russian history. 'To separate the Russian state from the church means separating the people from its conscience' was the general opinion among the ecclesiastical hierarchies.[4] By contrast the Bolsheviks argued that religion belonged to the private sphere, fighting against the church as an expression of the *ancien régime* which the Revolution sought to destroy and as an ideological adversary.

In 1917, for the Russian church the bond with the state had not signified submission. The convocation in August 1917 of the Local Council of the Russian Orthodox Church allowed by the provisional government, after the refusal by the Tsar to approve a request put forward by the majority of bishops since 1905, had led to the re-establishment of the patriarchate after more than two centuries. In the council, a great church, with a complex structure, rich in cultural, theological, spiritual and pastoral ferment, pledged to a work of profound renewal, regained its independence from the state.[5]

The re-establishment of the patriarchate and the new canonical order indubitably reinforced the church. Regular canonical structures were rebuilt, and at the centre of the church a visible hierarchy was renewed which was to play a fundamental role throughout the Soviet period, proving, despite many difficulties, an important factor of unity. The patriarchate represented the visible expression of canonical legitimacy and the unity of the church, which were the two main and complementary preoccupations of the Russian church during the Soviet experience. The challenge was to avoid a ruinous division evoking the unresolved drama of the schism of the seventeenth century, and to preserve those minimal structures which, once freedom was regained, could guarantee a basis for rebirth.

The anti-religious policy between ideology and bureaucracy

At the beginning of the 1920s, when the civil war was over, the church emerged as the main opposition force in the USSR: the anti-religious policy then took on great importance for the Soviet government.[6] The programming and the implementation of this policy underwent various phases and involved different strategies. One constant was the plurality of structure and organisms of the Soviet power. In the first place there was the Communist Party, working above all through the Department of Agitation and Propaganda of the Central Committee, which formed the centre of the strategic development and co-ordination of the anti-religious policy. Secondly, there were the instruments of government established from time to time to implement the political lines, which also exerted influence in phases of development. Finally, there were the security organizations with their various names (Cheka, GPU, OGPU, NKVD, KGB). These had a primary role in the implementation of the anti-religious policy, even if often it is not easy to reconstruct it.

It is difficult to reconstruct in detail the terms of the political debate within the system of Soviet power. The same thing also applies to the anti-religious policy.[7] At all events, however, it is possible to identify two basically different approaches, though these are often co-existent and complementary. One is ideological and the other is bureaucratic, and they correspond to two features which characterize the Soviet experiment in a more complex way.

The ideological assumptions of the Soviet state determined an approach which was radically antagonistic to the religious factor. In the Soviet Union, no form of anti-clerical lay secularism was in fact applied. On the contrary, an attempt developed to realize a utopia with eschatological features, marked by the absolute and omnicomprehensive characteristics of a real religious faith. Various aspects of the Soviet experience can be seen as an attempt at a 'religious' sacralization of the Communist state.[8] The ultimate object of the 'theology without God' of Soviet religion consisted not only in the annihilation of the church but also in actually taking its place.

On the other hand, over the years, the Soviet state came to be constructed as a complex bureaucratic machine which claimed to control the whole of society, bringing it within the framework of a socialist legal system. Therefore in the Soviet apparatus there was also a diverse approach to the anti-religious policy: without questioning the ideological postulates, it favoured the application of a rigid bureaucratic and administrative control to the ecclesiastical structures in the form of a campaign of systematic attack on the church.

The choice of loyalty to the Soviet state

The famous declaration of loyalty to the Soviet state made in 1927 by Metropolitan Sergi (Stragorodsky) has been considered by many people to have been a vile compromise with the atheistic powers by the church and a denial of what many suffered for through the persecutions.[9] In reality the declaration was in substantial continuity with the line adopted by Patriarch Tikhon, not without dignity, in 1919 and more clearly in 1923. After having been arrested in 1922 for resistance to the cruel campaign of confiscating the possessions of the church, and having been made destitute and reduced to the lay state by a self-proclaimed minority council, convened with the support of the GPU by the schismatic group of innovators of the 'Living Church', the patriarch declared the loyalty of the church to the state. That was the real turning point in relations with the Soviet power, which showed itself inexorable to a church which did not intend to submit. The Bolshevik experiment had been translated into a stable government: should the Russian church have taken the option of becoming clandestine? The political option of Tikhon and then of Sergi was that of arriving at a compromise to find a *modus vivendi*.

It is appropriate to try to understand the motivation which led the heads of the Russian Orthodox Church to make this choice. The fear of a ruinous internal division is a key feature for understanding the lines of conduct adopted by the patriarchal church. Tikhon and his successors regarded the danger of schism as the main threat to the survival of the church.[10] In 1925, after the death of the patriarch, power in the church passed into the hands of Sergi, Metropolitan of Nizhny Novgorod, the substitute for the last of the three *locum tenens* of the patriarchal throne designated by Tikhon, who had all been arrested. The government veto on the election of a new patriarch, the weak canonical legitimation of Sergi's direction and the impossibility of exercising it fully because of the continual arrests to which Sergi himself was subjected, did not favour the maintaining of links between the various components of the church and its centre. The fear of disintegration was not unjustified, above all after a new schism appeared, provoked by the agents of the GPU, called the 'Gregorians'. This strengthened Sergi's conviction that a recognition of the church government by the state would reinforce the weak centre of the church and guarantee its unity. But the legalization could be granted by the Soviet authorities only on condition of a substantial acceptance by the church of a relationship of submission to the state.

Metropolitan Sergi was arrested for the fourth time after a secret attempt to elect the patriarch and after presenting to the government a declaration in which in addition to affirming loyalty, in defence of the rights of the church he affirmed the incompatibility of Christianity and Marxism and asked the government to observe the law on separation by abstaining from interfering in the internal affairs of the church.[11] Under the threat of the execution of more than 110 imprisoned bishops, Sergi resolved to publish a declaration in which he affirmed in the name of the church: 'We want to be Orthodox and at the same time to recognize the Soviet Union as our civil fatherland, whose [i.e. the fatherland's] joys and successes are our joys and successes and whose failures are our failures.'[12] The step was difficult and full of suffering: the head of the church made compromise over the denunciation of persecutions and the defence of the rights of the church a priority, thinking that this was the best, if not the only, way of guaranteeing the survival and the unity of Russian Orthodoxy. Looking at subsequent years it can be claimed that the declaration did not bring great advantages to the church. In 1929 a new campaign began against the church which led to the mass persecutions of the 1930s.[13]

We must remember that in 1927, although the church had already undergone numerous violations, it was not easy to foresee what direction it should have taken in the events of the 1930s. In 1927 Soviet society was still living in the climate of the New Economic Policy, and numerous encouraging signs of liveliness could be seen within the life of the church.[14] It was possible to hope for peaceful coexistence with the Soviet state.

The 'Great Patriotic War' and Stalin's concordat

The Second World War marked a fundamental turning point in the Soviet experience of the Russian church. At the beginning of the war the church had been greatly weakened by the great persecutions which had struck it throughout the 1930s. In the territory of the Soviet Union, only a few hundred churches remained open, and in many provinces there was not even one; in large cities like Odessa there was not a priest who could celebrate. On the eve of the Second World War only four bishops were at liberty in the Soviet Union: the possibility that the visible presence of the Church of Russia would disappear was not unrealistic.[15] For the church of the 'enemies of the people' the war represented a great occasion for re-entering the heart of the Russian nation. Faced with the enemy invasion and the intense sufferings caused by it, to some degree a Russian national unity was restored, and a sense of continuity with the history of Holy Rus'.[16] The adjectives 'great' and 'patriotic' which were applied to the war in Soviet rhetoric were in fact a response to the authentic sentiments of the Russians and a large part of the Soviet peoples. The activity of the church during the war years was characterized by a sincere patriotic pledge to sustain the war against the invader. The joys, the successes and the failures in the 1927 declaration became an expression which matched up with reality.

On the other side, the official ideology during the war took up the themes of the Russian Christian tradition. A church allied with the life of the country regained a significant place. On 4 September 1943, on the eve of the Teheran Conference, Stalin received Metropolitans Sergi, Aleksi (Simansky) of Leningrad and Nikolai (Yarushevich) then of Kiev, subsequently Krutitsky, at the Kremlin. The Soviet dictator, wanting a second front to open up soon in the West, had had to listen to the requests for religious freedom coming from the governments and public opinion of the English and American allies; on the other hand it is not out of place to suppose that Stalin was also preoccupied with presenting a new image of the USSR, no longer an enemy of religion, as part of broadening his own zone of strategic influence over the countries of Eastern Europe. The 1943 meeting, on the basis of a revaluation of the Russian national factor, was the seal on an unwritten concordat between Stalin and the church. The state granted the church the right to convene the council to elect the patriarch and to regain a sphere of activity, albeit limited.[17] For its part the church assured the state of its loyalty and collaboration, in particular in support of the interests of Soviet foreign policy and foreign propaganda.

For the three metropolitans, brought up with the idea of a monarchical Russia or a Russia which was in some way Orthodox, to recognize the Soviet Union as their own state had been the product of a laborious itinerary, a journey in search of a place in which the church could survive. Sergi had been a protagonist at the stage of ecclesiastical ferment in the pre-Revolutionary years and the council of 1917–1918. Aleksi and Nikolai were expressions of this church. It was a church of great personalities who had not fled from suffering and had also personally shown their own fidelity to the patriarchal church (all three metropolitans had suffered arrest or exile in the 1920s), towards the re-establishing of which they had contributed. In their eyes the patriarchate represented the only possibility of the rebirth of true church life. For Sergi to be received at the Kremlin, in the palace of the power which had sought to annihilate the church, and to be given the possibility of electing the patriarch, was a success arising from the political suffering which had begun in 1923.

The improvement in relations with the Soviet state had contributed to the almost complete reabsorption of the schisms formed in Russia in the 1920s and 1930s, to the recovery of the parishes and the dioceses of the territories which had been outside the frontiers of the USSR after the First World War, and to a return to the jurisdiction of Moscow of major parts of the church of the emigration. Furthermore Stalinist policy had liquidated the Greek Catholic Church in West Ukraine, the historical Uniate enemy of the Russian church, giving the patriarchate an undeniable advantage. In the context of the 'National Bolshevism' with which Stalinist post-war policy was coloured, and with the recovery of some traditional 'imperial' interests of Russian policy, the church had been stimulated and supported by the government in a revival of secular aspirations to be the soul of Slav Orthodoxy and to challenge Constantinople for the role of centre of reference for the Orthodox world. Although the operation did not succeed completely, 'in the period after the Second World War Orthodox Moscow became a religious pole of universal breadth, with a capacity for attraction in the Christian world. The prestige of Orthodox Moscow is surprising for anyone who in 1939 noted the low state of religion in the USSR.'[18]

Collaboration with the 'controller-persecutors'

The Soviet state did not cease to exercise control over the church. The new state organization instituted by Stalin in 1943, the Council for the Affairs of the Russian Church, exercised control with rigour, and the KGB continued its work. Such a situation was inevitable within the Soviet state. The church worked in an obligatory system of relationships with a state which was 'persecuting' or 'controlling', and always hostile towards the religious factor. The new system guaranteed the church a living space, albeit a minimal one, and the situation was incomparably better than the cruel persecutions of the 1920s and 1930s. If the church wanted to exist as a visible presence in the Soviet Union it was obliged to work within this system. The acceptance of such a condition has seemed to be the expression of an attitude of collaboration. However, the question was not always whether or not to collaborate with the structures of power, but very often how, within the rules of the system, to use the inevitable bonds with the institutions to seek places of freedom and the good of the church. In some sectors of Russian Orthodoxy, however, from the middle of the 1960s a movement of ecclesial dissent from the patriarchate began to appear, which accused it of accepting a system of relations with the state which was contrary to the authentic interests of the church.

The line taken by the instruments of control and repression went through various stages. The Council for the Affairs of the Russian Orthodox Church, under the direction of G.Karpov, an official of the NKVD nominated by Stalin as president of the organization in 1943, pursued, though in a context of substantial state control of the church, the role of a link between the party and the state on the one hand and the ecclesiastical hierarchy on the other. This guaranteed relations as far as possible a character of 'co-operation'. The objective was to normalize relations between the state and the church and to hold the patriarchate to patriotic positions. However, the Khruschchev period coincided with a recrudescence of the anti-religious campaign, within an ideological scheme of a transition from the socialist phase of the Revolution to the Communist phase, during which all the remnants of the bourgeois and capitalistic past were to disappear. The 'Cold Persecution', practised with administrative systems and methods applied with a pedantic bureaucratic zeal, led to a marked restriction in the space available to the church between 1958 and 1964.[19]

The new orientations broke the pact between the church and the state, provoking a lively reaction from Patriarch Aleksi and Metropolitan Nikolai. The latter was removed from his post and died after less than a year. At the beginning of 1960, Karpov was replaced as president of the council by V.Kuroedov, a Communist apparatchik from the Department of Agitation and Propaganda. In conformity with the new orientation, he exercised control over the church with the aim not so much of normalizing relations as of progressively limiting the space in which the church could operate. If Karpov had sought a relationship of 'co-operation' with Aleksi, Kuroedov brought mutual relationships back into the clear confines of a submission of the church to the state. In 1961, Patriarch Aleksi was forced to convene a council which approved a reform of the status of the parish, entrusting all the powers to the laity of the parish council, of whom the parish priest became a dependent. With the fall of Khrushchev the attack on the church lessened, but the basic emphasis given to the relationship between the Council for Religious Affairs and the Orthodox Church remained essentially unchanged until the years of perestroika.[20]

A 'Sovietized' church

If despite the decades of persecution the church remained a point of reference for the major parts of the population, atheistic propaganda and the role played by the schools in the Sovietization of the new generations led to the formation of a *homo sovieticus* who was atheistic or at any rate agnostic, generally ignorant of religious questions. The pressure exercised by the state on categories which had any social relevance kept whole sectors of society away from church life. The church again lost contact with the intelligentsia and with the most active sectors of society. The churches were mainly attended by old women, on whose shoulders fell the weight of the transmission of the faith.

There was a profound change in the church in the 1950s and 1960s arising from a change of generations, but also from a break with those who had had experience of the conciliar period, the time before the Revolution. Because it was largely the victim of the persecutions or had emigrated, there was no generation to hand on the heritage of this church which was so rich in ferment and which had experienced the council and the bloody persecution by the state of its successor. A new type of bishop and priest was trained, for the most part born and educated in the Soviet period. These men had found their own ways towards conversion to Christianity, ways alien to the traditional Orthodox formation. Most of the time the question of loyalty to the Soviet state did not arise for them in the terms in which it had arisen for the previous generation.[21] For the new ecclesiastics, Soviet citizens trained in the totalitarian regime, loyalty to the state was an acquired attitude. At all events, for good or ill, the Soviet Union was their state: the question whether or not to recognize it had no foundation as such, as it did for the previous generation. The new bishops and the new priests did not ask whether or not they should accept the prevailing system of relations between church and state, because they were aware that to violate it would have meant a forced abandonment of the church. The challenge was how to build the church in the conditions of the Soviet system.

The challenge of modernity

The controversial figure of Metropolitan Nikodim (Rotov) is crucial for understanding the fortunes of the Russian church in the 1960s and 1970s.[22] Nikodim was an expression of the new generation: he grew up in the Soviet period, the son of a provincial secretary of the Party, and was converted in adolescence. He was nominated bishop in 1960 at a very early age (thirty-one), became president of the foreign relations department of the patriarchate and soon afterwards Metropolitan of Leningrad. Nikodim, unlike the preceding generation of bishops, considered the foreign relations of the church not so much a price to be paid in the framework of the concordat with the state as an activity proper to the church, which had to pursue its own interests, linking them with the directions of Soviet foreign policy. International activity made it possible to reinforce the prestige of the church by giving it greater power *vis à vis* the state. At the same time Nikodim sought to bring the Russian Church out of isolation and insert it into a framework of ecumenical organizations and bilateral relations which 'compelled' it to engage in dialogue and encounter with the other churches.[23]

The Soviet persecution had abruptly interrupted the work of renewal which Russian Orthodoxy had begun to pursue from the beginning of the century and which had first been implemented in the council of 1917–1918. This effort had been undertaken in a stimulating encounter with the beginning of the modernization of Russian society. After the Revolution, the modernization of society and the life of the church had gone two distinct ways. Russian society modernized itself through the Soviet experiment, while the church, caught in the jaws of persecution, on the one hand underwent an alienation from the process of the modernization of society and on the other made the defence of tradition a fundamental factor for its survival, emphasizing its traditional conservatism. The fate of the Living Church, which had put forward some of the most radical ideas of the pre-conciliar period, had the effect of compromising the reforming authorities, complicating the already difficult relationship between tradition and renewal which had characterized the history of Russian Orthodoxy.[24] The nature of the church increasingly came to be identified with tradition and was dissociated from the reforms. The break in generations which had characterized the Russian church in the post-war period did not favour the overcoming of the opposition between church tradition and renewal or that between Orthodoxy and modernity.

In the second half of the 1960s and in the 1970s a new interest in the church made itself felt in the Russian intelligentsia and beyond; this led to a significant number of conversions. There was a need to find a new synthesis between church tradition as now understood and the demands of renewal made by a new generation which had not formed in the tradition of the church. The theological academy of Leningrad, which underwent notable development under the impulse of Nikodim, became a decisive centre for relations between the church and those sectors of the Soviet intelligentsia which were close to it.[25] The Metropolitan, skilfully exploiting his links with the state apparatus, succeeded in getting round the law, unwritten but strictly observed, which did not allow anyone with higher education or sons of the intelligentsia to go to the theological academies, and in the course of the 1970s allowed numerous young people from the intellectual classes to enter the academy. The ecclesial experience of Nikodim's experiment, with an eye to the relationship between the Russian church and modernity, represented an attempt within the church of those years to restore the combination of church tradition and renewal, orthodoxy and modernity.

Perestroika, the Millennium of the Baptism of Rus' and Russian identity

With the advent of Gorbachev's reform policy of perestroika, as is well known the conditions of life in the church also changed: the church progressively regained its freedom. This process was accompanied with the reopening of churches, monasteries and seminaries and by a significant religious revival in the population. The council convened in 1988 approved a new statute for the church, drawing its inspiration from the decisions of the 1917–1918 council. On 30 January 1991 the church was finally given the status of a person recognized under law by the Soviet government.[26]

The rebirth of the church accompanied the revival of Russian national identity, which had begun to develop notably from the end of the 1970s and the early 1980s. The solemn celebrations of the Millennium of the Baptism of Rus' held in 1988, which in the eyes of the Soviet and international public was the symbolic image of the rebirth of the church, at the same time constituted an affirmation of the indissoluble link between the identity of Russia and the history of its church. The ceremony of swearing in the new President of Russia, B. Yeltsin, elected by universal suffrage in June 1991, was the symbolic representation of a new evaluation of the links between the Russian state and its church on the basis of a renewed sense of national identity. Alongside the President sat the new Patriarch of Moscow, Aleksi II (Ridiger), elected by secret ballot of the Council of the Russian Church in 1990.

In the course of the Soviet period the patriarchate had to some degree been the guarantee of the continuity of Russian history. In the conciliar consciousness of 1917 had been rooted the conviction that with the monarchy fallen and the army divided, the patriarchate represented the only institution which could express the unity of the Russian people.[27] The head of the church at a time of disorder could appear as a 'living representative of the national life', a defender of the 'idea of national and religious unity'.[28] The awareness of being the guardian of Russian identity had been a characteristic feature of the consciousness of the church during the Soviet period. In the conciliar assembly of 1917 this consciousness was echoed in a solemn way in the words of Archimandrite Ilarion (Troitsky): 'In Jerusalem there is the "wailing wall"... In Moscow in the cathedral of the Dormition there is also a Russian wailing wall – the empty patriarchal throne... They call Moscow the heart of Russia. But where does the heart of Russia beat in Moscow? ... Certainly it beats in the Kremlin. But where in the Kremlin? In the district tribunal? Or in the military barracks? No, in the Cathedral of the Dormition. There by the first column on the right should beat the Orthodox heart of Russia.'[29] On 19 August 1991, while the tanks of those involved in the coup were going into action on the streets of Moscow, Patriarch Aleksi II was celebrating the liturgy of the feast of the Transfiguration in the Cathedral of the Dormition in the Kremlin. Symbolically, on a day which was crucial for the birth of the new Russian state, the patriarchate of Moscow had regained its ancient place at the heart of the palaces of Soviet power.

Out of isolation

In the Soviet years a process of encounter between Russian Orthodoxy and the Christian West developed which involved the church of Moscow in a network of ecumenical links and relations. It was perhaps the very conditions of its life in the Soviet Union which obliged the church to seek external contacts. Under the pressure of persecution, Patriarch Tikhon on many occasions turned to the heads of the Christian churches to ask for their solidarity, and the numerous appeals on the Russian church's behalf addressed to the Soviet government by political and religious figures, including the pope and the Anglican primate, led to its freedom from arrests.[30] In the period after the Second World War the plan of the Soviet state to exploit the church for its own foreign policy was certainly a key factor in leading the church to be open internationally. However, the Russian churchmen also had an authentic interest here, as happened in the 1940s or in the period in which foreign relations were carried on by Metropolitan Nikodim. It could seem that support for the foreign policy of the USSR was the main task of the Russian churchmen in ecumenical relations: but one could ask whether, given that they were representatives of a church and of a culture of which an unbreakable bond between church, national identity and state was so prominent a feature, one could ever envisage them being engaged in international activity not only against the foreign policy of their own country, but also in a way independent of it.

Here we have examined a complex and contradictory development which at any rate has prompted the patriarchate of Moscow to come out of the isolation and self-sufficiency of the local church in an encounter with the experiences of the other churches, even if this has not always been easy. In a contribution to the 1917–1918 Council, Serge Bulgakov presented a broad vision of the role which the patriarchate could have played in the future of the Russian church:

> Unlike the Rus' of Moscow, where the patriarchate was an instrument of excessive national isolation, now for us the patriarchate is the organ of the universal awareness of the Orthodox Church, which the provincial college of the synod could not have been. The patriarchate is the head of the church, which raises itself above local limits, sees the other summits and is seen by them... We live in an age in which the narrow and provincial existence of the local church has become impossible, since a series of questions is arising which are not only international but also interconfessional in character.[31]

Bulgakov's conception of the patriarchal institution was integrated with the conviction that Orthodoxy, as a national church, should have a particular status of *primus inter pares* in the Russian state in that it was 'thus organically joined to the people, its culture and its statehood, which it is now longer possible to separate from the social organism which is the national state'.[32] The culture of the 'national church' and aspiration to a 'universal consciousness' are terms which have been integrated differently in the course of the history of Russian Orthodoxy, and which after the collapse of the Soviet Union and the birth of the New Russian state are continuing to have a central place in the Russian ecclesial awareness.

If the testimony of so many martyrs and the handing down of the faith of the church to the new generations are a precious legacy of the Soviet experiences, the laborious quest for a new ecclesial synthesis between traditions and renewal, between national identity and universal vocation, between roots in the land and an overcoming of isolation and self-sufficiency are a major part of the heritage which the generations of Russian Christians who have experienced the most difficult Soviet years are handing on to the churches of the West and to the new generations of the Russian Orthodox Church.

Notes

1. For the history of the Russian church in the Soviet period cf. N.Struve, *Les Chrétiens en URSS*, Paris 1963; J.D.Pospelovsky, *The Russian Church under the*

Soviet Regime 1917–1982 (2 vols), New York 1984, and above all the edition in Russian brought up to date on the basis of new documentation, *Russkaya pravoslavnaya tserkov' v XX veke* (The Russian Orthodox Church in the Twentieth Century), Moscow 1995; J.Ellis, *The Russian Orthodox Church*, Keston College 1986. For the period between the Revolution and the end of the Second World War see also L.Regel'son, *Tragediya Russkoi Tserkvi 1917–1945*, with a postscript by I. Meyendorf, Paris 1977, Italian translation *La tragedia della Chiesa russa 1917–1945*, with an introduction by G.Capara and a note by A.Rudnev, Milan 1979.

2. S.Bulgakov has written that 'the ecclesiastical consequences of the Revolution have an unparalleled importance for the history of Russia': S.Bulgakov, 'The Old and the New. A Study in Russian Religion', *The Slavonic Review*, March 1924.

3. A.Shmemann argues that 1917 'brings to an end a whole epoch in the history of Orthodox itself', *Istoricheskii put' pravoslaviya* (The Historical Way of Orthodoxy), Moscow 1993 (first edition New York 1954), 341. For the synodical period of the history of the Russian church see A.V.Katrashev, *Ocherki po istorii russkoi tserkvi* (Essays on the History of the Russian Church) II, Paris 1954, reprinted Moscow 1991, 311–557.

4. Cf. Pospelovsky, *Russkaya pravoslavnaya tserkov' v XX veke* (n.1), 445 n.3.

5. The Russian church in 1917 numbered 117 million faithful, 67 eparchies, 130 bishops, more than 50,000 priests and deacons, 48,000 churches, 58 seminaries, more than 1,000 monasteries and around 95,000 monks and nuns.

6. For the Soviet anti-religious policy see *Religion and the Soviet State: A Dilemma of Power*, ed M.Hayward and W.C.Fletcher, London 1969; J.D.Pospelovsky, *A History of Soviet Atheism in Theory and Practice, and the Believer* (3 vols), London 1987–88; B.R.Bociurkiw, 'The Formulation of Religious Policy in the Soviet Union', in *Readings on Church and State*, ed. J.E.Wood Jr, Waco, Texas 1989, 303–18; M.Odichev, 'Khozdenie po mukam' (The Way of Calvary), *Nauka i religiya* 5, 1990, 8–10; 7, 56–7; 8, 19–21; V.Alekseev, *Shturm nebes otmenyaetsya? Kriticheskie ocherki po istorii bor'by s religiei v SSSR* (Has the assault on the heavens been stopped? Critical essays on the history of the struggle against religion in the USSR), Moscow 1992; *Religious Policy in the Soviet Union*, ed. Sabrina Petra Ramet, Cambridge 1993; J.Anderson, *Religion, State and Politics in the Soviet Union and Successor States*, Cambridge 1994.

7. See the different arguments on this topic by B.Bociurkiw, 'The Shaping of Soviet Religious Policy', in *Problems of Communism*, May–June 1973, 37–51, and Anderson, *Religion, State and Politics in the Soviet Union* (n.6), 17–19.

8. One might think of the Soviet monumentalism, in the sense of the sacrality of power; of the creation of Soviet 'sanctuaries' (Red Square, Lenin's Tomb); of the symbolism of mass demonstrations and of the introduction of Communist rites.

9. After the declaration and the legalization of the synod formed by Sergi, there were some 'right-wing' schisms within the patriarchal church promoted by those bishops, often prisoners in the camps, who did not recognize the validity of the synod formed by Sergi or did not share the line expressed by his declaration. The majority of the bishops who separated from Sergi in these years came to be reconciled with him after his election as patriarch in 1943, or with his successor Aleksi (Simansky). However, the synod of Karlovci, which had given life to the schism of the Russian Orthodox Church abroad (which still exists), remained firm in its anti-patriarchal positions. Cf. D.Pospelovsky, 'Mitropolit Sergiy i raskoly sprava' (Metropolitan Sergi and the Right-Wing Schisms), in *Vestnik russkogo khristianskogo dvizheniya* 158, 1990, 53–81.

Although the Church of the Innovators did not gain a great following among the faithful, it was largely welcomed by the married clergy, and represented a serious danger to the church, considering that in 1926 the Church of the Innovators numbered 84 dioceses and around 11,000 priests and deacons and that from 1922 to 1927 the supreme council of the church, made up of innovators, was the only organ of ecclesiastical power recognized by the state.

11. This first declaration by Sergi was close to the spirit of the message sent to the Soviet government in May 1926 by the bishops imprisoned on the Solovetsky islands. The text of the message of the bishops and the project of the declaration by Metropolitan Sergi are in Struve, *Les Chrétiens en URSS* (n.1), 293–305.

12. With a play on words the Metropolitan had aptly linked the joys, the successes failures to the word fatherland and not to the Soviet Union; he complained to a metropolitan who came to visit him from abroad in the 1930s that no attention had been paid to this detail. Cf. the text of the declaration in Struve, *Les Chrétiens en URSS* (n.1), 305–9.

13. In addition to the studies already cited see N.Werth, 'Le pouvoir soviétique et l'Eglise orthodoxe de la collectivisation à la Constitution de 1936', *Revue d'études comparatives Est–Ouest* 24, 1993, 3–4, 41–9.

14. In those years there was a development of Christian youth groups, of lively parish communities and of theological conversations which lasted well into the 1930s. There were also some attempts to open institutions of theological training, and the church drew closer to some sectors of the intelligentsia. In the 1937 census more than half the Soviet population had declared itself believing. The matter was kept a close secret.

15. To gain some idea of the dimensions of the persecutions it should be noted that in all, from 1918 to the end of the 1950s they caused the death of around 3000 bishops (including those of the Church of the Innovators, which was also persecuted in the 1930s), more than 50,000 priests and a large number of the faithful, which is difficult to calculate.

16. Cf. S.Averintsev, 'Noi e la gerarchia, ieri e oggi', *La nuova Europa* 2, 1933, 1, 28. See the whole article, which is an important contribution to reflection on the Soviet experience of the Russian church.

17. In 1943, the council elected the Metropolitan Sergi patriarch; on his death in 1945 Metropolitan Aleksi (Simansky) was elected. In 1948 the episcopate of the Russian church in the Soviet territories numbered 70 members and 85 monasteries were open with around 4,600 monks and nuns; in 1950 it proved that in the territories of the Soviet Union 14,344 churches were open and 13,483 priests were active; 8 seminaries were functioning and 2 theological academies with 585 and 145 students respectively, and some publishing activity had been resumed.

18. A.Riccardi, *Il Vaticano e Mosca, 1940–1990*, Rome and Bari 1992, 59. Riccardi's study provides an important framework for the fortunes of the Russian Orthodox Church in the years of the Cold War within the dynamic of international relations and relations between the Churches. Cf. also W.C.Fletcher, *Religion and Soviet Foreign Policy 1945–1970*, London 1973.

19. The persecution led to the closure of a large number of churches (in 1959 only around 1300 were open, in 1965 only 7,000) and monasteries (in 1969 there were 69 and in 1965 only 17), while only 3 seminaries and 2 theological academies remained open.

20. In 1965 the 'Council for the Affairs of the Russian Orthodox Church' was unified as the 'Council for Affairs of Religious Worship', which was concerned with all the other

religious confessions; it formed a new 'Council of Religious Affairs' of which Kuroedov was president until 1984.

21. An authoritative Muscovite priest, Vsevolod Shpiller, who before the war had lived in the emigration in Bulgaria, noted such a change in the new generations of bishops and priests, cf. Pospelovsky, *Russkaya pravoslavnaya tserkov' v XX veke* (n.1), 293–4.

22. In 1970 Patriarch Aleksi I died, and in 1971 Metropolitan Pimen (Izvekov) of Krutitsky was elected Patriarch by the Council of the Russian Church.

23. Cf. Riccardi, *Il Vaticano e Mosca, 1940–1990* (n.18), 285.

24. In addition to all the works on the Russian church already cited here, for a deeper understanding of the schism of the Innovators, also in relation to the reforming current present in the Russian church at the beginning of the century, see C.Gousseff, 'Le schisme rénovateur: un mouvement pro-communiste dans l'Eglise russe', *Revue d'études comparatives Est-Ouest* 24, 1993, 3–4, 9–28; D.Pospelovsky, 'Obnovlenchestvo, Pereosmyshlenie techeniya v svete arkhivnykh dokumentov' ('The Schism of the Innovators. A Revaluation of the Tendency in the Light of Archive Documents), *Vestnik russkogo khristianskogo dvizheniya* 168, 1993, 197–227.

25. See the interesting reconstruction of the history of a group of Leningrad intellectuals who converted to Christianity between 1965 and 1975 in N.Sacharova, 'Rendere visibile il volto autentico della Chiesa russa e udibile la sua voce', in *I Politica nell'Est. Una lettura critica del ruolo dei cristiani nel sociale e nel politico*, ed. Centro Aletti, Rome 1995, 227–54.

26. On 1 October 1990 the Supreme Soviet of the USSR approved the law 'On Freedom of Conscience and Religious Organizations', followed by the Supreme Soviet of the Federal Republic of Russia, which on 25 October adopted an almost identical law 'On the Freedom of Religious Confession'.

27. It should be remembered that the reference to the unity of the Russian people in the ecclesial consciousness of Muscovite Orthodoxy was made in the perspective of the Rus' of Kiev, often also including the Byelorussians and the Ukrainians. The 1917 Council of the Russian Orthodox Church adopted for the patriarch the title, still maintained, *of svyateishii patriarkh moskovskii i vseya Rusi* (Most Holy Patriarch of Moscow and of all Rus'), which is usually translated as 'Patriarch of Moscow and of All Russia', with reference to Great Russia, Little Russia (Ukraine) and White Russia (Byelorussia). For the significance of the institution of the patriarchate in the history of the Russian Church see *IV Centenario del'istituzione del patriarcato in Russia*, Rome 1989.

28. Such words were used by Prince E.Trubetzkoi, a Russian theologian allied with V.Solovyev, speaking in the conciliar discussions on the question of the re-establishment of the patriarchate, cf. *Deyaniya Svyashchennogo Sobora Pravoslavnoi Rossiiskoi Tserkvi 1917–1918 gg.* (Acts of the Most Holy Council of the Russian Orhodox Church 1917–1918) II, Moscow 1994 (first edition Petrograd 1918), 28 (19 October 1917), 308. Among other things Trubetskoi underlined the importance of its role of the patriarchate if at the end of the war part of the Russian population found itself in the territory of other states.

29. Ibid., 29 (23 October 1917), 383. The place of the patriarchal cathedra is by the first right-hand column of the Cathedral of the Dormition. Ilarion (Troitsky), theologian, Professor of the Theological Academy of Moscow, Archbishop of Berezhsk, Vicar of Moscow and a close colleague of Patriarch Tikhon, died in a camp in 1929.

30. For relations between the Russian Church and the Holy See during the pontificate of Benedict XV see R.Morozzo della Rocca, *Le nazioni non muoiono. Russia rivoluzionaria, Polonia indipendente e santa Sede*, Bologna 1992.

31. S.Bulgakov, 'Smysl patriarshestva v Rossii' (The Significance of the Patriarchate in Russia), in *Deyaniya Svyashchennogo Sobora Pravoslavnoi Rossiiskoi Tserkvi 1917–1918 gg* (Acts of the Most Holy Council of the Russian Orthodox Church 1917–1918), III, Petrograd 1918, 31, now in *Akty svyateishego Tikhona, patriarkha moskovskogo i veseya Rossii, Pozdneishiie dokumenty i perepiska o kanonicheskom preemste vysshei tserkovnei vlasti 1917–1943* (Acts of the Most Holy Tikhon, Patriarch of Moscow and all Russia, Later documents and correspondence on the canonical succession of the supreme ecclesiastical power 1917–1943), Moscow 1994, 26–7.

32. Pospelovsky, *Russkaya pravoslavnaya tserkov' v XX veke* (n.1), 36.

The Fruitfulness and Contradictions of the Russian Emigration

Nicolas Lossky

To understand the complex picture offered by the Russian emigration in the twentieth century, particularly in its canonical organization, which is full of contradictions, we need to begin with a brief account of the prehistory that we find in America. In fact we have to go back to the eighteenth century and the evangelization of the Indians of the Aleutian Islands and Alaska by the Russian monks who came down as far as California in the wake of the trappers and fur merchants (Fort Ross, founded in 1812). This missionary action gave rise to a diocese which little by little extended all over America; its seat was transferred to New York in 1905. This Russian diocese, granted broad internal autonomy, welcomed the Orthodox of all races who emigrated to the USA and Canada. Here was the beginning of the organization of a peculiarly American Orthodox Church which was strongly encouraged by Tikhon, the Archbishop of America. This situation lasted until 1917.

In 1917, a local council of the Church of Russia met in Moscow. All the bishops attended it. Tikhon (canonized today) was elected patriarch. The Revolution prevented the sending of a new bishop to America and when finally, in 1923, Patriarch Tikhon was able to nominate Platon as metropolitan, the latter found a completely new situation. Between 1917 and 1922, each of the principal Orthodox Churches of the world had claimed its 'nationals' and established its own jurisdiction over them. Instead of the unity of all the Orthodox of America which prevailed until 1917, the Orthodox found themselves divided into a multiple of parallel jurisdictions based on their ethnic origin. So it is America which first offers the picture of jurisdictional divisions, contrary to Orthodox ecclesiology; these were to develop in what has come to be called the 'Diaspora' and in particular in the Russian emigration.

If for America the Bolshevik Revolution had been the catalyst – to some degree accidental, at least to begin with – of a situation representing an important contradiction in the emigration in relation to Orthodox ecclesiology, this was not the case for Europe. Here we have to remember the role that imperial Russia played in the eyes of the majority of Orthodox in the world. By virtue of its power, it appeared as a kind of protector of all the Orthodox Churches, a kind of continuation of the Byzantine empire, the Orthodox ideal of earthly existence (but without laying claim to any kind of primacy which would rival Constantinople; here there is no question of the famous notion of 'Moscow the third Rome' – we should not forget that the Russian church lived under a 'synodical' regime, since the patriarchate had been abolished by Peter the Great – but simply of a great political power, rich and protective. The important number of traces of the generosity of the Tsars in the Holy Land are sufficient illustration of this situation, and we should remember the traditional privileged relations between, for example, Russia and Serbia.)

What would seem important here is to understand that the Revolution affected the whole of the Orthodox world and, of course, the Russians first and foremost. Several questions arose with the fall of the last Orthodox empire, questions which divided the Russians both in Russia and in the emigration.

The first of these questions was whether it is possible for the church to exist without an emperor on the throne. Today this question might seem naive, but in reality it was not. Behind this naive question was a more basic twofold question:

(*a*) To what degree is the existence of the church bound up with the presence of a recollection of the imperial Byzantine ideal? If the reply to this question was an unreserved no among the best spirits who, from the beginning of the century, had been preparing actively for the Council of 1917, for some the presence of an emperor seemed indispensable. Thus those who were detached from the Russian Church at the beginning of the 1920s, later to become the 'Russian Church without frontiers' (1921–22), expressed this conviction at the beginning of their existence.

(*b*) The other more general aspect of this question was whether the earthly existence of the church was or was not bound up with a given socio-political system or whether the church could exist with any of these systems, even if it was violently anti-religious and anti-Christian in particular, and persecuted the church. Here, too, the Russians were divided into those for whom the church could not co-exist with an atheistic persecuting state and those for whom the church has the duty to remain present in any political situation, no matter what. The emigration divided on this point in 1931 when the vast majority, with its bishop Metropolitan Eulogius, left the jurisdictional obedience of the Church of Russia, which was judged to have compromised too much with the Soviet state. The hierarchy sought the recognition of this compromise from emigrants, and called for asylum with the Patriarchate of Constantinople. The small minority which remained faithful to the Patriarchate of Moscow refused to leave, saying that one leaves one's bishop only for reasons of heresy.

As a result, from 1931 the Russian emigration, the majority of which was concentrated in Paris, was divided into three jurisdictions which were not in communion with one another: the so-called 'Synodical' Church or 'Russia without Frontiers' (or 'Karlovtsians') formed in the 1920s (its seat is now in New York); the 'Exarchate or Ecumenical Patriarchate for Russian Parishes' (now the 'Archdiocese of France and Western Europe', the seat of which is still in Paris); and the 'Exarchate of the Patriarch of Moscow' with a seat in Paris (now suppressed as an exarchate in Europe and divided into several territorial dioceses: France, Great Britain, Belgium, the Netherlands).

Another aspect of ecclesiology has from the beginning been a factor of division within the Russian emigration, above all in Europe. This is the question whether Orthodoxy is identified with a given culture, in this case Russian culture. Since they have been uprooted from the natural environment within which they had hitherto practised their Orthodoxy, the emigrés and exiles (some of whom left of their own accord and others of whom were expelled) have been obliged to raise this question. For some the answer has been simple: one is Orthodox because one is Russian, so one is Russian before being Orthodox. Among these, some thought that the Soviet 'episode' would not last and that they were only abroad for a short time. Consequently, for them it was necessary to preserve a quite traditionally Russian Orthodoxy and they had a tendency to organize a kind of 'ghetto' life, whether in Europe or America.

For others, and this leads us to some degree from the contradictions of the emigration towards its fruitfulness, the vision of the relationship between Orthodoxy and Russianness has been quite different. They have not interpreted their presence abroad as a simple accident of history. For them, uprooting has been an occasion for discovering that their Russianness could be a source of wealth called to a fertile encounter with other cultures, and that their Orthodoxy came before their Russianness. The result of this was that if Orthodoxy was not necessarily bound up with a given culture (Russian, Greek, Bulgarian, Serbian, Romanian, Arab, and so on, which had long been Orthodox cultures), this Orthodoxy could express itself in any culture without exception, including Western culture.

For many representatives of this tendency this notion was strongly reinforced by the recognition, notably in France, of being in a very ancient Christian country and having a long common period (of at least a millennium) within one and the same Church which some love to call 'undivided'. This discovery has led these Russian emigrés to ask themselves the most fundamental question of all: what is the true and profound nature of Orthodoxy? One of the most prestigious representatives of this tendency, Fr Serge Bulgakov, wrote right at the beginning of the 1930s in his book *Orthodoxy*: 'Orthodoxy is the Church of Christ on earth. The Church of Christ is not an institution but the new life with Christ and in Christ, moved by the Holy Spirit.'

It is clear that with such a 'definition' of Orthodoxy, which quite naturally implies a permanent distinction between the essential and fundamental – Christ himself and the holy Spirit – and the secondary – the culture and forms of expression of this fundamental – the men and women who belonged to this current of emigration very soon came into deep contact with the other Christians – Catholics, Anglicans and Protestants – in the countries where they found themselves.

It is out of this recognition of the mobility of the heritage of the best that Russia had produced in the nineteenth and the beginning of the twentieth centuries that the St Sergius Institute of Orthodox Theology in Paris was founded in 1925. The heritage in question was constituted by what is usually called the Russian 'religious renaissance', with thinkers like Aleksi Khomyakov or Vladimir Solovyev in the nineteenth century. In the twentieth century this renaissance continued with men like Fr Serge Bulgakov, a brilliant theologian who has already been mentioned, philosophers like Nicolas Berdyaev, Simon Frank, Nicolas Lossky and others. But there is another thread to the heritage which also began in the nineteenth century and flourished in the twentieth: the rediscovery of the fathers of the Church. From the middle of the nineteenth century, editions and translations of the Fathers and studies of them could be found in the theological academies of Russia. The two men who made this heritage fruitful in the twentieth century were Fr George Florovsky and Vladimir Lossky (older son of the philosopher). I say 'made fruitful' because these two men (paradoxically, both 'amateur' theologians; they did not study theology in the classical sense) were not content to know the Fathers and make them known; they brought about a revival of the true vocation of Orthodoxy, namely a living patristic theology. In this perspective it is not enough to cite the Fathers; one has to have the same ecclesial experience of God as the Fathers. In other words, there has to be a recognition that one is called to be the Fathers of the church for one's time, that is, to proclaim for today, in today's categories, the essential of what has been received from the witnesses of all times: 'Jesus Christ, the same yesterday, today and for ever' (Heb.13.8).

One interesting case is that of Paul Evdokimov, who has achieved something like a synthesis between the heritage of Russian religious philosophy and the rediscovery of the Fathers of the Church.

Younger theologians, like the late Fr John Meyendorff and Fr Alexander Schmemann, have pursued and developed this rediscovery of patristic theology. Fr Schmemann, a great liturgist, gave liturgy new life by inaugurating a new approach that is now called 'liturgical theology'. It is not just a matter of taking the well-known adage l*ex orandi – lex credendi* very seriously (and quite naturally vice versa: the rule of prayer cannot in any case be out of accord with the rule of faith), but also of understanding that the structures of the offices have a theological lesson to offer us.

Fr John Meyendorff, who died prematurely in July 1992, was a Byzantinologist, a church historian and a theologian with a world reputation and of exceptional brilliance. Unfortunately he did not have time to realize his important project of adapting his work to the service of Russia after the liberalization. This Russia has great need to be illuminated by the best of the fruitfulness of the emigration, and Fr John Meyendorff seemed likely to be the best person to achieve this important work.

Furthermore Frs Meyendorff and Schmemann have been the true architects of the Autocephalous Orthodox Church in America. This church is an eminently live church with a liturgical life full of meaning, stripped of the accretions and distortions (like the way in which the community finds it impossible to hear the eucharistic prayers and other things) that one still finds throughout Orthodoxy today. Both were trained at the Institute of St Sergius in Paris and they took the best that this Parisian emigration had to offer to the Orthodoxy Seminary of St Vladimir in New York, which they entirely renewed and stamped with their luminous personalities. The Orthodox Church of America (OCA) is present in the USA, Canada and Latin America.

The fruitfulness of the Russian emigration has also made itself felt in other very important spheres of Orthodoxy. These include the rediscovery of the theology of the icon after a long period of decadence, with the Paris iconographers and theologians Leonide Ouspensky and the monk Gregory Krug, both of whom made what had begun in the 1920s at Prague in the 'Seminarium Kondakovianum' bear fruit. In an order of ideas quite close to iconography and iconology, the Russian emigration has also given new birth to an approach to liturgical music which is at once more traditional and more theological. If this renaissance began with the foundation of the

Institute of St Sergius and one of its main founders, Michel Ossorguine, the work and reflection have been continued and been developed strongly by Maxime Kovalevsky, who was without doubt the most brilliant composer of liturgical music in the Russian emigration. His destiny is interesting, since while remaining very Russian, he has devoted his life to a French expression of Orthodoxy.

All these forms of fruitfulness – and, it must be confessed, some of the contradictions – of the emigration which have been mentioned here are being pursued today by men and women who are often remarkable. However, as will have been noted, I have refrained from mentioned those who are still alive.

So I shall end simply by saying that in my view the most important fruitfulness to which the Russian emigration has given rise and which could bear very rich fruit today is a very serious involvement in the ecumenical movement, both in bilateral and in multilateral dialogues. The Orthodoxy that the Russian emigration has shown to world Orthodoxy is particularly suitable for a fruitful ecumenical dialogue, since it is an invitation, first for the Orthodox themselves and then for all the others, to a permanent conversion to an Orthodoxy which is always purified, and thus to a rediscovery of the common roots of all Christians.

II · *Vis à vis* the West: Approach and Rejection

Ecumenical Relations with the Orthodox Churches of the East from a Viennese Perspective

Franz Cardinal König

A key experience

It was February 1960. At that time I had been Archbishop of Vienna for four years, and Cardinal Stepinac, Archbishop of Zagreb, had recently died, an exile in his own country, after a long imprisonment. When I read the obituary I said to myself: in normal times the Archbishop of Vienna would quite naturally go to a funeral in Zagreb. But Tito's Iron Curtain between Austria and Yugoslavia made this impossible at the time, above all for a bishop. So I resolved to ask the Yugoslavian Embassy in Vienna for an entry visa for the funeral on 13 February 1960. This, I told myself, would be refused; but it would give me the opportunity to explain publicly how I had wanted to go to the funeral but had not been given an entry visa. To my great surprise and quite unexpectedly, however, I was informed that the Yugoslav embassy would grant me an entry visa for this purpose. I therefore set off on the afternoon of 12 February, spent the night in Graz, and had no difficulty in crossing the Yugoslavian frontier in the early hours of the next day. I and my secretary had a serious car accident near the small town of Varazdin. Badly injured, I was taken to the hospital in Varazdin. For the following days the only decoration on the white walls of my sick room that I had to look at was the famous photograph of Marshal Tito.

The thought occurred to me at the time: what is the significance of this accident for my life? In that hospital a notion emerged which in some respects was to govern my later life: the Archbishop of Vienna should have some concern for the persecuted bishops and dioceses just beyond the frontiers of the East. This thought kept pursuing me during my later years.

And what then happened was perhaps also governed by my stay in that hospital.

1. Austria and the churches of the European East

Austria has preserved its centuries-long experience as a state of many peoples even after the collapse of the monarchy in 1918. In the period after 1945, Austria was squeezed between the two opposing alliances of NATO and the Warsaw Pact, often becoming the point of encounter between East and West. Its neutrality, itself a product of the Cold War, was extremely helpful here. At this time Vienna proved itself as a third seat of the United Nations and as the host for an important part of the Organization for Security and Cooperation in Europe.

This situation could be utilized not only for politics but also for the encounter of the churches of the East and West in general and of Orthodoxy and Catholicism in particular. Just to mention a few dates: the first contacts with Orthodox Christians of the Patriarchate of Constantinople go back to the twelfth century; after the conquest of the city in 1453, many Greeks came to Vienna. In 1555, 1000 copies of the New Testament in Aramaic were printed for the Syrian Patriarch of Antioch. Austria was also the first Catholic state to organize an autocephalous, independent, state and national church on its territory. The Patriarch of Pec, who had fled from the Turks at the end of the seventeenth century, was welcomed, along with his faithful, in Austria and was recognized as head of all the Orthodox on Austrian soil. The later Patriarchate of Karlowitz was the spiritual centre for the Orthodox of the monarchy and the meeting point of Russian, Greek and Western cultural influences.[1]

From the seventeenth century onwards, Armenians from the Ottoman Empire also came increasingly to Austria. The Greek Cathedral of the Holy Trinity was built in Vienna in the eighteenth century and initially served Greeks and Romanians (Wallachians) as a place of worship (from this century on, Galicia, Siebenbürgen and Bukovina came under Austrian administration). When diplomatic relations between Russia and Austria began under Tsar Peter I, a house church was built next to the Russian embassy. The Cathedral of St Nicolas was consecrated in 1899, and since 1946 Vienna has been the seat of a Russia Orthodox bishop. The Orthodox of Dalmatia, who for a while were under Venetian and then under Austrian rule, and from 1873 were subject ecclesiastically to the Metropolitan of Czernowitz, also often held their annual synod in the Greek church in Vienna. In 1880, a concordat with the Ecumenical Patriarchate in Constantinople was made for the Orthodox of Bosnia and Herzegovina:

where the young theologians did not study at home in the seminary in Ráljevo, they were sent to Athens and Khalki. So old Austria was in constant contact with prominent places of Orthodox theology. Catholics and Orthodox, Latin and Byzantine Christians have achieved a peaceful co-existence. The Austrian Habsburg empire – as it would be called today – was ecumenically wide open to the Orthodox churches.

The tensions between East and West after the Russian Revolution and especially after the Second World War made further fruitful dialogue difficult. The common battle by the capitalist West and the Marxist East against the Nazi dictatorship could only rise above the political opposition for a while. An iron curtain descended over Europe. However, this curtain did not seem to be totally impermeable. On the side of the Catholic Church the turning point came with John XXIII, when as recently as under his predecessor Pius XII the Decree against Communism had marked a spiritual highpoint in the church's defensive war.

John XXIII was interested in a dialogue. He was the also the one who led me to be involved in the church's relations with the East as one small cog in the machine. On one of my audiences with him he invited me spontaneously to visit Cardinal Mindszenty in his exile in the US Embassy in Budapest. When I objected that this might not be so easy, he replied: 'What's difficult about it? Go to Vienna station, buy a ticket to Budapest and get on the train' – and laughed. Now I went by car, not by train, but that one time became many.[2]

Travels to Poland, Hungary, Czechoslovakia, Romania and Yugoslavia followed.

The Archbishop of Vienna is the Western bishop nearest to the East, and I saw that as my legitimation. Moreover I repeatedly noted that even today – more than seventy years after the end of the Habsburg monarchy – Vienna has a good reputation with the peoples of the East. Even the youth, who want to know nothing about old times, link certain expectations, hopes and dreams with the name of Vienna. For the bishop from neutral Austria it was at first easier to travel in a Communist country than for a bishop from a Nato state.

Small Austria does not just owe its revival to the collaboration of East and West; it can only exist if there is peace in Europe and if relations between East and West are peaceful.[3] Though contact with the Catholic Church under Communist rule is different from contact with the Orthodox churches, time and space remain the same. 'Since for geographical, historical, psychological and political reasons access to the East seems easier from Vienna than from any other city, and as Vienna is the place which is easiest to reach from all the Orthodox church centres, what is more natural than that the Archbishop of Vienna should offer his services for making contacts with the Church in the East?'[4] Furthermore, many Western churches are represented in Vienna by a permanent pastor or a bishop. There was a good ecumenical climate here which encouraged many kinds of links with the Orthodox.

Looking again at the present we can see today, after the end of the Cold War, that we are facing a changed situation in church politics. With the fall of the Berlin Wall and the Iron Curtain in 1989, the collapse of the Soviet Union and the dissolution of the Warsaw Pact, Europe has entered on a new phase of history. By comparison with the military and political blocks which stood facing each other, much that had become fossilized is moving again. States have disappeared from the map and others have taken their place, some of them unstable. Not only hopes and perspectives, but also a loss of orientation and anxiety about the future arise from this. New possibilities of spiritual and political exchange are overshadowed by the flaring up of intolerant nationalism and armed conflicts. Europe again is the scene of war.

Reflecting on its historical roots, Austria, now a member state of the European Union, must issue a warning that Europe is more than the community of Western industrial states. Here the churches have an important role and can provide an impulse towards integration. The World Council of Churches in Austria and the Austrian Conference of Bishops of the Roman Catholic Church want to give a significant sign in this respect in 1997. They have invited the Christian churches of all the countries of Europe to meet in Graz from 23 to 29 June 1997, where together with the Conference of European Churches and the Council of European Conferences of Bishops, the second European Ecumenical Assembly will take place, seven years after the Basel event. In accordance with the new facts in Europe, the assembly theme of 'reconciliation' is intended to make a valuable contribution to the growing together of Europe.

II. The Viennese local church in dialogue with the Eastern churches – Pro Oriente

On the basis of the special presuppositions mentioned above, Vienna has proved to be a place of encounter and dialogue with the churches of the East. As earlier as 1964, two weeks before the third period of the Second Vatican Council came to an end with a passing of the Decree on Ecumenism, *Unitatis redintegratio*, on the basis of various advice, I decided to found Pro Oriente in Vienna.[5]

The purpose of Pro Oriente as laid down in its foundation document is: 'To nurture and advance ecumenical relations between the Roman Catholic Church and the Orthodox, pre-Chalcedonian and pre-Ephesine Churches, to deepen ecumenical reflection in Austria and support ecumenical activities between Christians.'[6] Sections of Pro Oriente which were set up by the local bishops in Graz, Salzburg and Linz made much wider and more intensive work possible in ecumenical relations with the Eastern churches.

As the founder of Pro Oriente I thought it important to point to the possibilities of a local church *(ecclesia particularis)* in connection with the world church. At that time I said:

> It was of providential significance that as a diocesan institution – and therefore primarily dependent on Rome – Pro Oriente looked to the non-Catholic church communities the other side of the then Iron Curtain, i.e. the so-called Eastern bloc. This church sphere was at first difficult for Rome and therefore lay in the lee of Roman interests. But Pro Oriente – and this is its merit – was able in later years to make valuable contacts with the ancient Eastern Churches on behalf of the Roman Secretariat for the Promotion of Christian Unity and do much in preparing the ground. There was less mistrust of 'Vienna' on the part of the conversation partner and his particular political situation than of Rome, the centre of the Catholic Church. So in the course of time metropolitans and patriarchs came form the sphere of the Syrian, Coptic, Ethiopian and Armenian churches. The 'Vienna Conversations' with the churches of the Byzantine tradition came into being – first of all again with the churches of the Eastern block from Romania, Bulgaria, Yugoslavia, Hungary and Poland.[7]

Similarly, Cardinal Willebrands, the former president of the Papal Council for the Promotion of Christian Unity, said:

> The universal church is present in its fullness in all local churches and is realized in the life of the local churches... The ecumenical dimension is one of the prime aspects of the life of the Catholic Church both on a world level and also at a local level. The Catholic principles of its ecumenical task... contain the requirement that the ecumenical initiatives should be adapted to local needs; for it is for the local church to make an indispensable contribution here in the midst of the reality of everyday life. But at the same time these principles constantly show us that any local initiative must be taken up without exception in such a way

that in it the community is supported in faith and in the discipline which makes the unity of the Catholic Church.[8]

That was the verdict of the Vatican expert on ecumenism, and he emphasized that the *'ecclesia particularis'* is the place where the universal church is at work in its fullness – in its responsibility for the whole church. Therefore with Pro Oriente to some degree an instrument has been brought into life which does justice to such responsibility in a particular way. In this sense Pro Oriente has collaborated closely with the Papal Council for the Promotion of the Unity of Christians.

Pro Oriente made a valuable contribution to dialogue with the ancient Eastern Orthodox churches which rejected the decision of the Council of Chalcedon (451). After a separation lasting more than 1500 years, in September 1971 in Vienna-Lainz there was a first – non-official – meeting of theologians of the ancient Eastern Orthodox churches and the Roman Catholic Church. Four more of these Vienna consultations took place in 1973, 1976, 1978 and 1988. The agreement worked out in Vienna made quite clear the unity in faith in Christ between the Eastern Orthodox churches and the Roman Catholic Church. This agreement in faith was also later incorporated into official documents: thus for example in 1973 in the joint declaration of the Coptic-Orthodox Pope Shenouda III and Pope Paul VI, in 1984 in the joint declaration between the Syrian Orthodox Patriarch Ignatius Zakka I Iwas and Pope John Paul II, and in 1990 in the dogmatic agreement between the Malankar Orthodox Syrian Church in India and the Roman Catholic Church. The ongoing unofficial dialogue with the Eastern Orthodox churches is now being co-ordinated by the Pro Oriente Standing Committee.[9]

In June 1994 it proved possible, with the help of Pro Oriente, to convene a first consultation of all the churches of the Syrian tradition.[10] Here dialogue was also entered into at an unofficial level with the (pre-Ephesine) Assyrian Church of the East. In the autumn of the same year Pope John Paul II and the Patriarch of the Assyrian Church of the East, Mar Dhinka IV, signed a joint christological declaration. Further non-official dialogue with the Churches of the Syrian tradition was planned with the Pro Oriente Syriac Commission, and continued in February 1996 with a second consultation at a high theological level.[11]

Pro Oriente was able to give important stimulus to dialogue with the Orthodox church of the Byzantine tradition. A first important step was my visit to Romania – I was the first Archbishop of Vienna and the first Cardinal of the Roman Church to do so. At this time relations between Rome and the Romanian church had been made difficult above all by the compulsory integration of the so-called Uniates in Siebenbürgen. The Romanian Orthodox Church rejected any direct contact with Rome, so it had no observers at the Second Vatican Council. Generally speaking, the start of theological dialogue was also blocked. My visit to Romania resulted in a return visit of Patriarch Justinian to Vienna in 1968. He was invited to preach at St Stephen's Cathedral in Vienna for the ordination of priests on the Feast of St Peter and St Paul. Further ecumenical hospitality, an exchange of priests and visiting lectures by theology professors made a new climate between the Roman and the Romanian church possible. This was also an important step towards the beginning of official dialogue.

A second important step in this direction was taken by an ecclesiological colloquium under the title 'Koinonia' for which Pro Oriente issued invitations in 1974. As early as 1964 the autocephalous and autonomous Orthodox churches had agreed in principle at their conference in Rhodes that joint theological dialogue should be entered into with the Roman Church, but felt that at that stage it would be premature. The churches of Romania, Antioch and Greece still had reservations.

The unofficial character of the colloquium in Vienna made it possible for theologians who also represented their church governments at pan-Orthodox conferences to take part and confer with Roman Catholic colleagues. The gathering was a success not only because prominent theologians of both church families were invited and took part, but finally also because the Secretariat for Unity and the Ecumenical Patriarchate in Chambésy helped to arrange the event. The President of the Papal Council for the Unity of Christians, Edward Cardinal Cassidy, also confirms that this dialogue, in which Orthodox theologians from Greece, Russia, Serbia, Romania, Poland and America took part,[12] was an important contribution to the start of official dialogue in 1980. The conversations of 1974 'proved to be a forum for a consideration of the events and steps which had led the church to the rediscovery of the bonds which unite the Catholic Church and the Orthodox Church. These conversations and contacts were certainly of inestimable value as preparation for the appointment of the Joint Commission for Theological Dialogue between the Catholic Church and the Orthodox Church.'[13]

Now we turn to contacts and exchanges with the Russian Orthodox Church.

III. Relations with Russian Orthodoxy

In February 1994, Patriarch Aleksi II wrote in his preface to the Pro Oriente Foundation book on a thousand years of Christian Rus' of the very fertile collaboration between the Patriarchate of Moscow and Pro Oriente:

> We are open to a brotherly dialogue with all those who come to us with pure intentions and are not practising open or hidden proselytism. From this perspective we attach very great importance to the ecumenical initiatives proceeding from the Pro Oriente foundation and its concern to make peace by resolving inter-confessional conflicts – for example in connection with the revival of the structures of the Greek Catholic Church in West Ukraine.[14]

The list of relations with the Moscow Patriarchate in the Pro Oriente Chronicle is a valuable demonstration of the variety of contacts.[15] These relations go back to the days of the Second Vatican Council.

The Russian Orthodox Church became more closely involved in ecumenical collaboration in 1961. With the entry of the Orthodox Churches of Russia, Romania and Bulgaria into the World Council of Churches at the New Delhi Assembly, new possibilities were also opened up for dialogue with Orthodoxy. 'Observers' from the churches of the World Council were invited right at the beginning of the Second Vatican Council and made an essential contribution to its ecumenical organization. Nevertheless the Ecumenical Patriarch of Constantinople initially refused to be represented at the Council, probably also having in mind the Russian Orthodox Church, for which journeys abroad were possible for the first time them.

Surprisingly, however, on the second day of the Council some representatives of the Russian Orthodox Church appeared in the Aula of St Peter's and by chance came into my hands. The surprise was all the greater, since it had been made known shortly beforehand that the Patriarch of Constantinople, as the one with the primacy of honour in the Orthodox churches, had refused to send representatives of the Orthodox churches. He did not think it opportune for Orthodox observers to take part in the great church assembly of the Roman Catholic Church. That was the first time that I met representatives of the Russian Orthodox Church.[16]

The Russian bishop resident in Vienna, Metropolitan Filaret Denisenko, had already taken part in the foundation of Pro Oriente in 1964. He had given a paper on 'Local Church and Universal Church' at an ecumenical symposium arranged by Pro Oriente in 1980. As later Metropolitan of Kiev and Galicia and as exarch of the Moscow Patriarch in the Ukraine, he was held in the highest respect in the Russian Church. He had given a festal speech at the 1988 Zagorsk Council. His deposition by the Russian Orthodox Synod in 1992 was unforeseeable in those early days. He is now Supreme Head of the Ukrainian Orthodox Church – Kiev Patriarchate – reorganized on his own initiative, but this is not recognized by the other Orthodox churches in communion with the Ecumenical Patriarchate.

From the beginning, Pro Oriente attempted to enter into ecumenical relations with the Russian Orthodox Church. Reciprocal visits were exchanged. Already in the 1960s representatives of Pro Oriente were received by Metropolitan Filaret in Kiev and Bishop German Timofeev of Tikhvin in Leningrad, and in the Spiritual Academies in Zagorsk and Leningrad; in June 1971 a Pro Oriente Delegation was received in the church foreign office of the Moscow Patriarchate by Archbishop Yuvenaly of Tula. The ecumenical climate in Vienna is characterized by mutual hospitality, visits of pastors to the Russian Cathedral in Vienna on their appointment and resignation, and joint participation in numerous ecumenical acts of worship and prayer.

Later it proved possible to invited distinguished theologians of the Russian church as speakers at ecumenical symposia and theological conference in Vienna. Already at the Seventh Pro Oriente symposium in Autumn 1969 Archpriest Vitaly Borovoi, at that time representative of the Russian Orthodox Church at the World Council of Churches in Geneva, gave a lecture on 'Ecclesiology and Ecumenism'. Bishop Melkhizedek Lebedev lectured in March 1970 on 'The Life of the Russian Orthodox Church'. At the Second Theological Conference Bishop German Timofeev spoke on 'The Development of the Idea of the Seat of Peter in the Pre-Nicene Period', and in May 1972 the outstanding theologian Archpriest Professor John Meyendorff considered the question 'When is a Council Ecumenical?'. So right at the beginning themes were discussed which have still not lost their ecumenical topicality and explosiveness today: primacy, ecclesiology, conciliarity. In addition, information was also given about the special spiritual depth and piety of the Russian Church. Similarly, in 1972 the patriarchal exarch in Western Europe, Metropolitan Anthony Bloom of Sourozh, gave a festal lecture for the fifth anniversary of Pro Oriente on the theme 'Orthodox Faith and Russian Spirituality'.

At the ecclesiological colloquium 'Koinonia' which has already been mentioned the Russian church was also represented by the participation of the Rector of the Leningrad Spiritual Academy, Archbishop Kirill Gundaev, and it had an active part with a lecture by the Rector of the Spiritual Academy of St Vladimir in New York, Professor John Meyendorff ('Sister Churches – Ecclesiological Conclusions from the *Tomos Agapis*').

In 1977, the then president of Pro Oriente, Theodor Piffl-Percevic, and the General Secretary, Alfred Stirnemann, were received by His Holiness Patriarch Pimen and the head of the church foreign office, Metropolitan Yuvenaly of Tula and Belev, in the synod hall of the Moscow Patriarchate. On this occasion Patriarch Pimen praised the ecumenical work being done from Vienna and encouraged the further continuation of these efforts.

One fruit of this patriarchal encouragement was a strengthening in relations with Metropolitan Filaret Vakhromeev of Berlin, exarch of the Russian Orthodox Patriarchate for Central Europe. He brought the congratulations of the Russian Church to the tenth anniversary of Pro Oriente and spoke in 1978 at the Twenty-First Ecumenical Symposium in Vienna on 'The Ecumenical Movement and the Russian Orthodox Church'. On this occasion, as Archbishop of Vienna I had an official part in the festal liturgy in the Russian Cathedral of St Nicholas in Vienna over which Metropolitan Filaret presided. He also maintained close links with the Foundation when he became Metropolitan of Minsk and White Russia and leader of the church foreign office. He also spoke in 1990, now as Exarch of the White Russian Orthodox Church, at the sixtieth ecumenical symposium in Vienna on 'The Present Situation of the White Russian Orthodox Church and its Prospects for the Future'.

Good relations are also being maintained between Pro Oriente and the successor of Filaret Vakhromeev: Metropolitan Melkhizedek Lebedev of Berlin was formerly Russian Orthodox Bishop of Vienna and Austria. In December 1979 Metropolitan Melkhizedek had given a lecture in Vienna on 'Pastoral Care in the Russian Orthodox Church' and in April 1984 reported to us on 'Ecumenical Dialogue after the Sixth Assembly of the World Council of Churches in Vancouver'.

Further ecumenical symposia were held in Vienna and contributed to a better mutual understanding. The illustrious host of speakers included, as I have said, Archbishop German Timofeev of Berlin, Metropolitan Irenej Susemihl of Vienna and Austria, Protopresbyter Vitaly Borovoi and Archimandrite Josif Pustoutov of the church foreign office in Moscow and the pastor of the Russian church in Vienna, Mikhail Turcin. The topics discussed always aimed at including the present situation in the lands of the Russian Orthodox Church. Some of them were: 'The Millennium of the Baptism of Russia' (1987), 'The Russian Orthodox Church under the New Conditions of Perestroika, Glasnost' and Democratization' (1990), 'Current Problems of Russian Orthodoxy' and 'Bilateral Relations between Rome and Moscow' (1994). The lectures were all published and in this form first made available to the German-speaking public. Pro Oriente also saw the publication of competent articles and discussions as a valuable means of ecumenical dialogue. Here are three examples, the topics of which directly relate to the Russian church.

Pro Oriente made an important contribution to a better understanding between Rome and Moscow by publishing a book on Pope John XXIII in Russian by the pioneer of Russian Orthodox ecumenism, Metropolitan Nikodim of Leningrad.[17] Metropolitan Nikodim visited Rome for the first time in 1963 and had expert knowledge of the Catholic Church. His book is now a textbook in the Spiritual Academies of the Russian Church. Mikhail Turcin comments:

> It is to be noted that at the time when Metropolitan Nikodim wrote the book there was unbridled atheistic propaganda in the Soviet press. The servants of the church were being slandered at every turn as scoundrels, as a relic of the past, as useless people in the new society, in the society of those who were building a bright future for humankind. Moreover many people had a completely false idea of the Roman Pope. Doubtless this was one of the fruits of the old form of education. And over against this caricature, created by the old ideas and the atheistic press, Metropolitan Nikodim set the real, true picture... This was also a special kind of defence of our spirituality, the spirituality of the Russian Orthodox Church, for at that time, under those conditions, there would have been hardly any other possibilities.[18]

On the occasion of the Russian Orthodox Council in Zagorsk (6–9 June 1988), Pro Oriente sent 500 copies of this book in Russian as a gift to all the members of the council and to the Spiritual Academies for their students and seminarians.

Two further important publications are the documentations of the major international academic Pro Oriente symposia 'Salzburg and the Mission to the Slavs – On the 110th Anniversary of the Death of St Methodius' (20–22 September 1985),[19] and 'A Thousand Years of Christian Rus'' (13–15 May 1988).[20] The second of these volumes contains not only the lectures given at the symposium, at which the Russian Church was represented by Archbishop Mikhail Mudyugin of Vologda, but also interesting documents relating to the 1988 Zagorsk Council, the jubilee celebrations of the millennium and relations between Rome and Moscow. 'This publication has scientific value first of all as a documentation of important events and writings from the years of the great Revolution in the former Soviet Union, 1988–1992. Some of these documents are clearly marked by the situation before the Revolution, some by the uncertainty of the revolutionary age, and others by the phase of the events of the Revolution.'[21]

Through this scholarly work at ecumenical symposia and by publications, Pro Oriente also seeks to indicate the cultural legacy of the Eastern churches and arouse understanding and interest in it. Among other things the Choir of the Russian Orthodox Patriarchate of Moscow has already twice been the guest of the Graz section of Pro Oriente (1990 and 1996), and on the initiative of the Salzburg section an exhibition was held in the Romanian Hall of the Archabbey of St Peter on the theme 'Heaven on Earth – Worship and Life in Orthodox Russia'.

I twice had the opportunity, as leader of a delegation of Pro Oriente, to take part in significant events of the Russian church: the 600th anniversary of the Battle of Kulikovo (1980) and the millennium of the Baptism of Rus' (1988). During our visit from 18 to 22 September 1980, His Holiness Patriarch Pimen of Moscow and All Russia received the Pro Oriente delegation.[22] This was the first time that an Archbishop of Vienna had visited the Russian Orthodox Church. In addition to the reception by the patriarch, conversations with representatives of the church foreign office, Metropolitan Yuvenaly of Krutitsy and Kolonna and Archbishop Chrysostom of Kursk and Belgorod, were also valuable. In Zagorsk the delegation was received by the Rector of the Spiritual Academy and took part in the festal liturgy of the Holy Synod in the Trinity Monastery of St Sergius on the occasion of the 600th anniversary of the battle of the Field of Kulikovo (*Kulikowo polye*).

At the invitation of the Russian Orthodox Church, with a delegation of Pro Oriente I took part in the festivities for the millennium of the baptism of Kiev Rus' (5–16 June 1988). During this visit to Moscow, Zagorsk and Kiev the representative of Pro Oriente were also observers at the Council[23] and took part in the patriarchal liturgy in the Yelokhovo Cathedral in Moscow which was celebrated by Patriarch Pimen.

On my last visit with a delegation of Pro Oriente in July 1991 to the Russian Orthodox Patriarchate there was an audience with his Holiness Aleksi II, and there were visits and conversations in Zagorsk and Minsk which were to develop trust between the Russian and Roman churches. Relations between Rome and Moscow were more intensive than ever before in 1989/90; but the readmission of the Catholic church on the territory of the former Soviet Union also made the climate much more difficult. Here respect for the Archbishop of Vienna and his Pro Oriente Foundation proved very helpful. The visit to Metropolitan Filaret Denisenko of Minsk was above all to help to clarify the difficulties that were developing in the Ukraine.

The visits by representatives of Pro Oriente in Lemberg in August 1993 and September 1994 were similarly eirenic. Conversations with representatives of the three disputed Ukrainian Orthodox churches – Bishop Augustin Markevich (Ukrainian Orthodox Church, Patriarchate of Moscow), Archbishop Petro Petrus (Autocephalous Ukrainian Orthodox Church) and Bishop Andrijk Gorak (Ukrainian Orthodox Church – Patriarchate of Kiev) – served as soundings in the confused situation and first attempts at mediation. The Pro Oriente book on a thousand years of Christian Rus' was presented to Orthodox and Catholic bishops. The reactions to it were of interest and very positive.

That brings us already to the future tasks which the local church of Austria and Pro Oriente Vienna with its Graz, Linz and Salzburg sections can perform for the Russian Orthodox Church.

Notes

1. For all this see F.König, 'Wien als Brücke zur Orthodoxie', in T.Piffl-Percevic and A.Stirnemann (ed.), *Ökumenische Hoffnungen. Neun Pro Oriente-Symposien 1965 bis 1970*, Innsbruck and Vienna 1984, Pro Oriente 7, 12–14.
2. F.König, 'Wien – Brücke zum Osten', in *Konziliarität und Kollegialität. Das Petrusamt. Christus und seine Kirche*, Pro Oriente 1, Innsbruck etc. 1975, 13.
3. Ibid., 16.
4. König, 'Wien – Brücke zum Orthodoxie' (n.1), 14.
5. Cf. O.Schulmeister, 'Wie es zu "Pro Oriente" kam – Zur Idee und Gründungsgeschichte des Stiftungsfonds', *Konziliarität und Kollegialität* (n.3), 20–4.
6. Cf. 'Chronik von Pro Oriente', in A.Stirnemann and G.Wilflinger (eds.), *30 Jahre Pro Oriente. Festgabe für den Stifter Franz Kardinal Konig zu seinem 90. Geburtstag*, Pro Oriente 17, Innsbruck and Vienna 1995, 278.
7. F.König, 'Die Ökumene heute', in R.Kirchschläger and A.Stirnemann (ed.), *Ein Laboratorium für die Einheit. 25 Jahre Pro Oriente 1989*, Pro Oriente 13, Innsbruck and Vienna 1991, 44.
8. J.Willebrands, 'Wie kann eine Ortskirche zur Annäherung zwischen der katholischen und der orthodoxen Kirche beitragen?', in A.Stirnemann (ed.), *Am Beginn des Theologischen Dialogs. FS T.Piffl-Percevic*, Pro Oriente 10, Innsbruck and Vienna 1987, 46.
9. The whole ecumenical dialogue with the Eastern Orthodox churches is analysed in D.W.Winkler, *Koptische Kirche und Reichskirche. Analyse von Schisma und ökumenischem Dialog* (preface by Franz Cardinal König), Innsbrück 1996 (forthcoming).
10. Cf. *Syriac Dialogue. First Non-Official Consultation on Dialogue within the Syriac Tradition*, Vienna 1994.
11. For all this see D.W.Winkler, 'Theologische Notizen zu den Ökumenischen Dialogen mit der Assyrischen Kirche des Ostens', *Ökumenisches Forum* 17, 1994, 243–66; id., 'Jüngste Entwicklungen in den ökumenischen Beziehungen der Assyrischen Kirche des Ostens', *Ökumenisches Forum* 18, 1995, 281–8.
12. All references and protocols have been published: Pro Oriente, *Auf dem Weg zur Einheit des Glaubens*, Innsbruck, etc. 1976; and *Koinonia. Premier Colloque*

ecclésiologique entre théologiens orthodoxes et catholiques, special issue of *Istina,* Paris (July 1975).

13. E.I.Cardinal Cassidy, 'Introduction', in A.Stirnemann and G Wilflinger, *30 Jahre,* Pro Oriente 8 (n.7).

14. Aleksi II, 'Preface', in A.Stirnemann and G.Wilflinger (eds), *Tausend Jahre Christliche Rus'. Zwischen Perestrojika und Ende der Sowjetunion,* Pro Oriente 15, Innsbruck and Vienna 1993, 9f.

15. 'Chronik von Pro Oriente' (n.7), 409–18.

16. F.König, 'Der russische Beitrag zum christlichen Europa', in Stirnemann and Wilflinger (eds.), *Tausend Jahre Christliche Rus'* (n.14), 24.

17. Metropolitan Nikodim Leningradsky, *Ioann XXIII, Papa Rimsky. Pobornik edinstva khristian* (with a foreword by Franz Cardinal König), Brussels 1984.

18. M.Turcin, 'Metropolit Nikodim und sein Buch *Johannes XXIII, Papst von Rom*', in A.Stirnemann and G Wilflinger (eds), *Tausend Jahre Christliche Rus'* (n.14), 177.

19. T.Piffl-Percevic and A.Stirnemann (eds.), *Der Heilige Method, Salzburg und die Slawenmission,* Pro Oriente 11, Innsbruck and Vienna 1987.

20. Cf. Stirnemann and Wilflinger (eds), *Tausend Jahre Christliche Rus'* (n.14).

21. P.Harnoncourt, 'Kirche und Kirchen in der ehemaligen Sowjetunion, Wissenschaftliche Erkenntnisse und neue Fragen', in ibid, 14.

22. Documented in Piffl-Percevic and Stirnemann (eds.), *Der Heilige Method* (n.21), 101–19.

23. Documented in Stirnemann and Wilflinger, *30 Jahre Pro Oriente* (n.7), 231–498.

Between Ostpolitik and Ecumenism: Relations between Rome and Moscow during Vatican II

Alberto Melloni

The Russian participation in the Second Vatican Council was an integral part of the identity of this assembly, which is the key event for Catholicism in the twentieth century. In the course of the years 1959–1962 (those of the preparation for the Council) and then in the years 1962–1965 (those of its effective development), the way in which the Church of Rome looked towards the Soviet capital and the way in which the Russian church regarded this solemn entry of Latin Christianity into ecumenism shaped a particular series of approaches, rethinkings and interpretations. Until a few years ago very little was known of all this: certainly Soviet diplomacy did not want to report what had been the expectations of the USSR in those years, while the patriarchate did not have even the minimal conditions for looking at that moment (and all the papers relating to it) with the necessary freedom. The reserve of the Secretariat of State at that time made it impossible to grasp the significance of the steps taken and the debate from which they had arisen. Therefore studies – of varied historiographical quality – passed rapidly over the topic of Vatican II and Moscow.

The limits of research up to 1978

One of the most well-trodden ways was to adopt an approach which isolated the events with a higher emotive content: a dignified and typical example of this is the attention paid by Giancarlo Zizola at the end of the 1970s to the pontificate of John XXIII.[1] The public signals of détente which the Pope and the Secretary of the Communist Party exchanged – greetings, messages of respect – did not modify the international political picture, but they did give the Council, which was being prepared for or begun, an unprecedented emotional dimension: the church, which seemed in fact to be laying down the weapon of severity,[2] discovered a new dimension of 'success', which grew out of understanding.

However, the complex 'liberation' of the Ukrainian Bishop Slipyj, long detained by the Soviet authorities, and the arrival at Rome of the first observers from the Patriarchate of Moscow in October 1962 – information about which also emerged, thanks to valuable documentary fragments made available by the secretariat of Pope John – did little to corroborate the commonplaces which had rapidly become encrusted upon Roncalli's pontificate. One side in fact read out of this sequence of facts the charge that the 'generosity' of the pope unblocked an anti-historical antagonism,[3] or concealed a plan that could not be divulged, which was to lead to agreement with the enemy by antonomasia.[4] This type of simplification, which cannot be dismissed because of the state of the documents, found other references. Another criticism was found in connection with the missile crisis which developed when a United States naval blockade prevented access to Cuba by a Soviet flotilla which was transporting components for the installation of missile ramps on the island. In the course of the tremendous strategic and military challenge which seemed likely to trigger off a nuclear conflagration, Pope John had decided to send a message to both the heads of state involved, John F. Kennedy and Nikita Khruschchev: with this gesture the Holy See broke with its unconditional support of the Western camp, which had lasted for decades, and regained a real neutrality for peace. However, this repositioning had distracted the attention of historians from the problem whether or not the pope had been effective in the past. In fact, while Khruschchev clearly attached some importance to the telegram sent by the Vatican,[5] the American administration was completely silent, except for a preoccupation with denying that the first and only Catholic President of the United States had obeyed an order of the Pope.[6]

Another event which has long been taken as a proof of Roncalli's 'weakness' or 'astuteness' was the visit of Aleksi Adzhubei and Rada Khrushcheva to the Vatican: the audience, granted on the eve of the elections in Italy in which the Italian Communist Party made a modest advance, was not only something for which the pope was 'reproved', but also thought to call for sanctions. That was so much the case that no one wanted to obey the pontifical order to publish the *nota verbale* of the meeting in the Vatican daily news: Pope Roncalli, who had grown up in the Curia of Pius XI, noted bitterly that in his time (as a young man) 'an order of the pope...'.[7]

Rhapsodizing (which was an option in a first phase of the publicity given to edifying collections of episodes) also remained a risk for successive historiographical criticism, starting from the researches of the historians of the ecumenical movement who were interested in the Council and its Muscovite echoes. No less than the history of international relations, this type of study, too, should have taken account of the limitations of the documentation, and also of the political effect of its own scholarly writing. In fact – up to the point of castigating the Council for Religious Affairs in the Central Committee of the Communist Party – the analysis of the complex dyschrony which is nevertheless decisive for the history of Vatican II, in the sending of the observers of the patriarchs of Constantinople and Moscow to the Council,[8] could not count on direct sources; moreover it had to take account both of the exposed positions of quite a few Orthodox prelates who were open to punishment or political pressure and of the lapse in studies on dialogue.

Recent contributions and perspectives of research

An improvement of quality became possible thanks to new sources which in turn became accessible in connection with the changes of policy both on the part of the Holy See and – while it existed – by the USSR. The election to the papacy in 1978 of a Polish cardinal put a 'subject' of the Warsaw Pact on the throne of Peter, and also marked the end of the Vatican so-called Östpolitik: rapidly what had been a line taken by the Secretariat of State has become the object of historical research.[9]

The progress in knowledge which has taken place in a little less than twenty years can be seen from a series of three important works which have appeared respectively in Germany (and the United States), in France and in Italy.

First of all Hans-Jakob Stehle, in the second half of the 1970s, chronicled Ostpolitik most meticulously and exploited the few documents then available to the full. His *Die Ostpolitik des Vatikans 1917–1975*, completed and enlarged in an English translation, has recently been further updated in a new German edition.[10] Stehele – who deals with the years of Vatican II but does not make them a specific theme – noted the transition which came about in the pontificate of John XXIII. He believes that he can recognize an analogy between Roncalli's line and 'the mystically-tinged dilettantism of d'Herbigny',[11] which I do not think exists, if only because of the abyss which separates the totalizing passion with which the Jesuit had flung himself in the direction of the Soviets in the 1930s from the bonhomie of the Vatican visitor and apostolic delegate, who had been able to observe Bolshevism first at work in Bulgaria and then by looking at Russia from Istanbul, the country of Trotsky's exile...[12] However, he is right in observing that what attracted the attention of the pope was the feeling that an impasse of perpetual indifference had been arrived at in relations between the Holy See and the USSR, and that was something to which Roncalli could not adapt in any circumstances.

What moved the Soviets, though, was a succession of three events: the papal audience of the Polish bishops on 8 October 1962, in the course of which the pope showed that he recognized the Oder-Neisse line; the statement by Monsignor Bengsch to the Central Preparatory Commission opposing the schema *De cura pro christianis comunismo infectis* of May 1962, in which he censured the propagandistic language disseminated in East Germany; and the papal intervention in the Cuba crisis of 24 October 1962.[13] The USSR retreated from this phase of détente – furthered by the activism of figures like Norman Cousins and Felix Morlion, representatives respectively of the world of culture and United States intelligence – when it was expecting to welcome the return of Pacelli's inflexibility with the advent of the Montini pontificate;[14] subsequently it resumed contact on a note which was instrumentally and strictly political and ideological. Leaving aside questions about the preciseness of such periodizations, it is a fact that according to Stehle the Council as such did not have any influence on Soviet-Vatican relations. There is nothing to suggest that its course could have had a specific significance in making possible anything that could not have been achieved by means of diplomatic relations, which were the means by which the 'normalization' of relationships was implemented from the 1970s on.

A few years after the appearance of the English edition of Stehle's monograph, the former director of *La Croix*, Antoine Wenger, a versatile and well-informed man, who had studied the relations between Rome and Moscow in the first half of the century,[15] described his experience in the church as a director of *La Croix* in a book entitled *Les trois Romes*. In a narrative similar to that of a diary, he describes the years of the Council in terms of relationships between the three patriarchates, and his periods of Vatican II divide up the whole work. Wenger begins by pointing out the contradiction between a commitment to *détente* and the internal repression by the Soviets, which reached a critical point in 1961, when in the full phase of the improvement of relations with Rome, the KGB imposed on the Russian synod the suppression of the canonical constitution of the parishes.[16] However, these are again impressions, often interspersed with the author's memories and the changes and hopes in relations between the churches.

A significant step was taken in 1992, with the appearance of *Il Vaticano e Mosca* by Andrea Riccardi.[17] The work of this Roman historian for the first time can draw on both Soviet sources and Vatican papers, or whole private dossiers of John XXIII. Above all for the years of the Council, Riccardi documents step by step how the flexibility shown to the West by the Soviet government was matched within by an aggravation of repressive anti-religious measures.

This is a dynamic which the Holy See did not recognize: basically the timing of Pope Ratti's condemnation of Bolshevism and the force of Pacelli's polemic had destroyed the two perspectives of Vatican diplomacy: 'the' Communist peril remained a static fact which did not get any better, though it did not get any worse. It was this immobility which broke in the years of John XXIII and the Council with an initiative made through the delegate to Ankara, Monsignor Lardone: in the direct colloquies in Turkey between this churchman and the USSR ambassador there the habits of traditional diplomacy were broken which judge the situation of a country by the respect in which its own ambassador is held. In John XXIII's words, a 'thread' was tied. The pope expected results in the long term; for the moment, however, this thread made it possible to remedy ignorance.

In Moscow, too, the ignorance of the other side was enormous: the Communist Party did not know its interlocutor; the Vatican question, passed by the Party authorities to the Ministry of Foreign Affairs after an intervention by the General Secretary of the Italian Communist Party, Togliatti, relating to Koslov,[18] was no less indecipherable for the Soviets. The illusion that the Vatican could be used by Communist diplomacy[19] to 'divide' the West was an approach which changed only as a result of contacts and the experience of the Council.

Stehle, Wenger and Riccardi thus make a significant contribution towards a progressive focussing of the characteristic features of the seven years of the Council: not that this was the objective, since there were also developments of great importance in the second half of the pontificate of Paul VI and the years from the election of Cardinal Wojtyla up to the disappearance of the USSR. Nevertheless it seems to me important to note how research has demonstrated the destructive impact of Vatican II on the ideological illusions of the protagonists in this area (and first of all on the mirage that the 'Neva and Volga, sooner or later, would flow into the Tiber'[20]). And what twenty years ago seemed a useful coincidence for a first periodization, appears on a renewed examination of the sources to be a causal relationship.

It would be aberrant to consider the Council to be the almost undeciphered appendix to a development extending over a long period,[21] or the basis on which an anachronistic history of the popes moves.[22]

The limits and the hypotheses of research

The political, diplomatic and religious changes which have taken place recently allow new investigations and give grounds for hope of further significant increase in research on relations between Moscow and Rome in the years of the Council. A first attempt in this direction was made at a recent academic colloquium held between 30 March and 2 April 1995, the proceedings of which have been published in a Russian edition in Moscow, in the Academy of Sciences series, and in Western languages at Louvain in the Bibliotheca Ephemerides Theologicae Lovanienses.[23]

In the gathering – part of the research programmes for the *History of the Second Vatican Council*[24] – it seemed necessary for the evaluation of the reciprocal influence of the Council on Moscow and vice versa to cover the whole range of subjects which each of the two terms comprises and the self-awareness of each side. This has brought out the differences between those involved and the interests at work in the capital of the USSR in the early 1960s and in the organs of the Orthodox Church. The latter, squeezed by unspeakable pressures and the temptation to follow them, tried also to look at the Catholic Council with a more specific interest. Despite the insuperable power of the propaganda machine and Soviet espionage, the Russian church maintained its own judgment in assessing Vatican II. It could not ignore the general political conditions – expressed in the views and the deliberations of the Party and in the lines adopted by the Minister of Foreign Affairs – but at the same time objectively opened a chapter of brotherhood between the churches, of which the Communist Party involuntarily became an interpreter.[25] The representatives of the Moscow Patriarchate at the Catholic Council were obviously approved and controlled by political and police organs but in the Aula of St Peter's they bore witness to the possibility of a true ecumenism.

Many people – during the Council and in research into it – have wanted to deny this difference and the plurality of meanings. There has been the traditionalist Catholic protest which has accused the Holy See of having 'bartered' the presence of the Russians for no further condemnation of Communism, or which has tried to reduce the presence of the Russian Orthodox in the Council to a gesture of arrogant benevolence on the part of the Soviet power, which was using its 'religious' hostages to deceive the church and the West, as if the power of the Communist Party had to fear that new condemnation which such bishops felt so important.[26] Now –

thanks also to the contributions in this volume – I believe that it can definitely be affirmed that this accusation can only be substantiated on the basis of an anti-Orthodox prejudice which find no echo in the sources. The long and important report on the visit of Willebrands which Cardinal Bea took to John XXIII on 7 October 1962, so far known only in fragments, clearly indicates that the invitation extended to Nikodim and the Russian synod had no political aims: at most it does not exclude the use of political instruments also in responding to the challenge that the Council objectively made to the ecumenical movement, which was called in those weeks to demonstrate its capacity to grow up.[27]

Thus purely on the Council side it has to be emphasized how various bodies and organs looked to Moscow in quite different ways, seeing it sometimes simply as the centre of an antagonistic and hated political system and sometimes as the seat of a difficult witness of faith and fidelity, and sometimes superposing the two things. But Vatican II and Moscow could not be examined in themselves and for themselves, cut off from a context – whether of ecumenism or of international relations – around which complex and decisive debates were developing. Therefore yet other elements – from the hypothesis of a further condemnation of Communism by the Council to the attitude of the ecumenical patriarch Athenagoras; from the attempts to come to grips with the idea of *sobornost'* by some important theologians of the Council to the role of the Communist Party of Italy (more preoccupied to show its own alignment than to inform) – have not seemed secondary, nor is it possible to ignore them.

An unexpected harmony

It is obvious that this is only the beginning of a new series of possibilities and prospects of historical research: research, even most recent research, is in fact incomplete in two ways, in respect of both methodology and subject matter.

On the one hand, in fact we must discount a methodological limitation of the subject matter. Thus, to take the case of the last volume cited, it is impossible to give a general account of ecumenical or political or diplomatic events *sub specie concilii*, nor should that be done: Vatican II is not the right 'spade' for excavating these documentary and political sites, nor is Moscow the right instrument for an exhaustive knowledge of the Council. Impatience here leads to recourse to guidelines alien to the sources.

On the other hand, there are topics which have remained on the periphery, but which could have made a contribution to historiographical comparison and progress in knowledge: the particular actions of the two pontiffs of the Council; the attitude of the diplomats of the Western countries, the Warsaw Pact and Cuba; the position of the Communist parties and the bishops of Eastern Europe; the respective judgments of the Communist parties in the West and the Marxist-Leninist liberation movements in the Third World; the attitude in the middle period of the ecumenical patriarchate and the World Council of Churches; the position of the Lutheran and Uniate minorities in this respect. These are themes which must be returned to or are already under discussion.[28]

However, while I am aware of these limits, I think that it is already possible to point to some quite new elements relating to studies of *Ostpolitik* and ecumenism in the years of the Council.

First of all it should be emphasized that an objectively paradoxical harmony emerges from meetings which brought together some sectors of the Roman Curia and the leading bodies of the Communist Party: both noted that the condemnation (or lack of condemnation) of Communism was an important theme in Vatican II.[29] The most specific dimensions of the Council – relating to liturgical renewal, ecclesiology and the Bible – remain secondary to this theme, which would later be pushed by Lefebvre's propaganda.[30] Even those like Gisueppe Siri, Cardinal of Genoa, who had made some small initiatives of their own in relations 'beyond the curtain', did not escape the ideological stereotype.[31] Symmetrically, in the Soviet reviews (including those in which there were some ideas that were not totally subservient to the demands of Socialist propaganda), the use of non-ideological categories in the approach to the Catholic council was unthinkable.

Secondly, I think that it can be asserted that recent research definitively lays to rest a myth bound up with the presence of the observers of the Russian church (and not the Greeks) at the end of the first period of Vatican II. The choice that the Roman invitation presented to Athenagoras (and on which he could decide autonomously, irrespective of the political power) was objectively difficult: the guarantees offered by the course of the preparation, the regulatory norms, the perception of the ecumenical qualities of the Catholic bishops, were such as to induce the *non possumus* of any synod. Even the Catholic theologians, before they began work, considered Vatican II irremediably in the hands of the dicasteries of the Curia:[32] *a fortiori* on the non-Catholic side, particularly out of love for the cause of Christian unity, it was sensible to ask whether perhaps it might not be more productive to have one's own observers in the East than to risk sending them and then having to recall them in conspicuous circumstances. It is precisely the absence of this scruple which allowed the Communist Party to force the hand of the Russian church[33] and issue the announcement that two observers from Moscow – already tried out in Paris in August – would arrive in Rome on 12 October 1962. It was gratuitous interference which saved the Pope, Bea and the Council (and also Athenagoras and Athenas) from repercussions the outcome of which are unimaginable.

Finally, it seems to me that all the studies presented show that from a political perspective the Soviet interest in the Council declined over time and that the Communist Party exerted no pressure nor even had any expectations in the direction of an endorsement by Vatican II of Pope John's opposition to the nuclear deterrent asserted in *Pacem in terris*. When Khruschchev, after the encyclical, asked in an interview reported in *Pravda* whether Kennedy and Adenauer would obey the pope's appeal for peace, he was expressing a short-term tactical position. In 1965, at the time when the decisions on the lawfulness and limits of war were more on the agenda in the final debate on the constitution *Gaudium et spes*, Soviet diplomacy no longer felt it possible to use the Council to divide the West.[34]

This was all the more the case since there was a common conviction in Western Europe that it was no longer possible to count on the Vatican for unconditional support of the anti-Communist policy which had now become part of planetary strategy. During the pontificate of John XXIII, whose 'ingenuousness' was regarded as dangerous weakening, this opinion spread, and it grew stronger in the first period of the pontificate of Paul VI. In Adenauer's judgment, even his election created a dangerous situation, and remedies were to be found on other levels. In a conversation with a French diplomat on the eve of the conclave in 1963 which refers to de Gaulle, he remarked:

> The policy pursued by the pope [John XXIII] since his advent seemed dangerous to him [viz. Adenauer] both for the West and for the future of Christianity. In other words, in evoking the possibility of a conclave he spoke with even more disquiet about Cardinal Montini, whose tendencies, he assumed, went further than those of John XXIII. His possible election to the pontifical throne would constitute a real danger to Europe.[35]

It is not easy to say whether Adenauer's position was an isolated one.[36] At any rate it is important to note that the hegemony of the ideological approach also extends to the sources as a veneer which needs to be analysed with great critical caution and then removed with critical 'solvents' which are not so mild as to be useless, nor so abrasive as to scratch the material.

I have tried to recontextualize in detail the situation in the first half of the 1960s, to fill the gaps in knowledge from which historiography has so far suffered, and to make more precise the instruments of research into Vatican II. At the same time this allows us to gain critical experience and factual elements which are also indispensable to those studying *Ostpolitik*; it is for them to seek to understand whether and to what degree the climate and experience that the conciliar Aula gave to diplomacy and ecumenism influenced events after 1965.

Notes

1. G.Zizola, *L'utopia di papa Giovanni*, Assisi 1978; in greater depth in the more recent *Giovanni XXIII. La fede e la politica*, Rome and Bari 1988.
2. The expression comes from the opening speech to the Council, in A.Melloni, 'L'allocuzione *Gaudet Mater Ecclesia* (11 October 1962), Sinossi critica dell' allocuzione', in *Fede, Tradizione, Profezia. Studi su Giovanni XXIII e sul Vaticano II*, Brescia 1984, 223–83.
3. Cf. e.g. E.Balducci, *Papa Giovanni*, Florence 1964.
4. Cf. the denigratory book by F.Bellegrandi, *Nikita Roncalli. Controvita di un papa*, Rome 1995. Similar ideological polemic has appeared in an edition of letters to members of the family during the years of the Second World War. It infers from some expressions of approval for Mussolini, contained in documents for which no degree of confidentiality was guaranteed, that Roncalli was a supporter of Fascism: for this see the introduction to *Lettere ai famigliari*, ed. G.Farnedi, Casale Monferrato 1994.
5. Quoted in H.Stehle, *Geheimdiplomatie im Vatikan. Die Päpste und die Kommunisten*, Zurich 1993, 427 n.43.
6. For the internal documents of the administration see A.Schlesinger, *A Thousand Days – John F.Kennedy in the White House*, Boston 1965, who cites the telegram from Bertrand Russell, but not the step taken by the Vatican! The family memoranda also maintain this line, as in John H.Davis, *The Kennedy Clan. Dynasty and Disaster 1848–1984*, London 1984, 362–3. In the absence of in-depth studies on the Kennedy and Rusk papers, scientific bibliography, e.g. G.Seaborg, *Kennedy, Khruschchev and the Test Ban*, Berkeley 1982, is not in a position to give satisfying results.
7. *Giovanni XXIII, Lettere 1958–1963*, ed. L.F.Capovilla, Rome 1978.
8. Cf. E.Fouilloux, *Les catholiques et l'unité chrétienne du XIXe au XXe siècle. Itinéraires européennes d'expression française*, Paris 1982; M.Velati, *Una difficile transizione. Il cattolicesimo e l'unità cristiana dagli anni Cinquanta al Vatican II*, Bologna 1996. For the positions in the preparation of the council cf. *Storia del concilio Vaticano II*, directed by G.Alberigo,*I, Il cattolicesimo verso una nuova stagione*, ed. A.Melloni, Bologna 1995.
9. For the line and the functioning of the Secretariat of State cf. A.Riccardi, *Il potere del papa da Pio XII a Giovanni Paolo II*, Rome and Bari ²1993; cf. further A.Wenger, *Le cardinal Villot 1905–1979*, Paris 1989; there are no studies on the activity of Agostino Casaroli from the reform of the Curia in 1968 to the end of the pontificate of Paul VI.
10. H.-J.Stehle, *Die Ostpolitik des Vatikans 1917–1975*, Munich and Zurich 1975;

English translation, *The Eastern Politics of the Vatican 1917–1979*, Athens and London 1981, extended to the whole Montini pontificate. See now *Geheimdiplomatie* (n.5).

11. Stehle, *Eastern Politics* (n.10), 301.
12. For this cf. F.della Salda, *Obbedienza e pace. Il vescovo A.G.Roncalli visitatore e delegato apostolico in Bulgaria 1925–1934*, Genoa 1988, and A.Melloni, *Tra Istanbul, Atene e la guerra. A.G.Roncalli vicario e delegato apostolico (1935–1944)*, Genoa 1993.
13. Stehle, *Eastern Politics* (n.10), 304–5.
14. Stehle finds significant the appeal by Ilychev, head of the ideological commission of the Communist Party, of 25 November 1963, which calls for the resumption of an intensive atheistic propaganda against the attempt of the ecclesiastical hierarchies to consolidate their positions in the face of Soviet kindness, cf. Stehle, *Eastern Politics* (n.10), 311.
15. A. Wenger, *Rome et Moscou 1900–1950*, Paris 1987.
16. Id., *Les Trois Romes*, Paris 1991, 113.
17. A.Riccardi, *Il Vaticano e Mosca*, Rome and Bari 1992.
18. Testimony by I.E.Karlov in the course of the seminar presenting Riccardi's volume *Il Vaticano e Moscow* at the Institute for Religious Sciences in Bologna, 5 May 1992.
19. It is in part the effect of the choice of the journalists and historians of the Italian Communist Party (G.Pierantozzi, P.Spriano and A.Salvati). Their reports and pieces, governed by attitudes with a very strong ideological alignment, became the basis of the reports sent to Moscow; for this see A.Agosti, *Togliatti*, Milan 1996.
20. For the formation of this illusion see R.Morozzo della Rocca, *Le nazioni non muiono. Russia rivoluzionaria, Polonia independete e santa Sede*, Bologna 1992, 340.
21. Cf. A.Tamborra, *Chiesa cattolica e Ortodossia russa. Due secoli di confronto e dialogo dalla Santa Alleanza ai nostri giorni*, Cinisello B. 1992, which end with a chapter on the 'Outcome of Vatican II', 437–50.
22. A volume by an Italian journalist who died prematurely, S.Trasatti, *La croce e la stella. La Chiesa e i regimi comunisti in Europa dal 1917 a oggi*, Milan 1993, has a place in this line. In it the ecumenical dimension does not have any other function than as a field of action for the pontificate.
23. This includes not only an introduction by the editor but also three groups of papers: (a) The level of international relations (Anatol A.Krassikov, 'The Second Vatican Council in the Context of the Relations between the USSR and the Holy See'; Victor Gaiduk, 'Vaticano e Cremlino. A proposito della presa di coscienza dell'ingresso nell'era nucleare "crinale apocallitico della storia"'; Valerij Liubin, 'Das Zweite Vatikanische Konzil und die wissenschaftliche Literatur darüber in der Sowjet Union'; Adriano Roccucci, 'Russian Observers at Vatican II: The "Council for Russian Orthodox Church Affairs" and Moscow Patriarchate between Antireligious Policy and International Strategy'; Nikolaij Kowalskij, 'Vatican II and its Role in the History of the Twentieth Century'; Jurij E.Karlov, 'Secret Diplomacy of Moscow and the Second Vatican Council'; (b) the level of ecumenism, Vitalij Borovoj, 'Il significato del Concilio Vaticano II per la Chiesa ortodossa russa'; Johannes Willebrands, 'Le rencontre entre Rome et Moscou: Souvenirs'; Mauro Velati, 'La chiesa ortodossa russa tra Ginevra e Roma negli anni del Vaticano II'; John Long, 'The New Relations between Rome and Moscow: First Reactions'; Emmanuel Lanne, 'La perception en Occident de la participation du Patriarcat de Moscou à Vatican II'; Antonella Cavazza, 'L'idea di *sobornost*' da A.S.Chomiakov al Vaticano II'; (c) the contours and debates

(Giovanni Turbanti, 'Il problema del comunismo e la Chiesa al Vaticano II'; Andrea Riccardi, 'Antisovietismo e *Ostpolitik* della S.Sede'; Valeria Martano, 'Il ruolo di Mosca al Vatican II vista ad Costantinopoli', 1959–1962).

24. The project, directed by G.Alberigo and by an international team of scholars, plans the publication of five volumes, of which two have already appeared, in Italy, the United States, Brazil and Portugal, France and Germany.

25. A comparison between the policies pursued by the Party in Russia and those in East Germany, Poland, Hungary and Czechoslovakia would be interesting here; this indirect encounter filtered by French diplomacy (which can be consulted in the archives of QO Paris, STS 1/2, 135) indicates a certain disparity between lines of conduct.

26. For this see the contribution of G.Turbanti above. There are no in-depth studies of the Polish episcopate and the other fathers from Eastern Europe for the conciliar phase; for the positions of the cardinal primate of Poland see the diary – limited to the parts relating to contacts with John XXIII – in S.Wyszynski, 'Byl Czlowik poslany od Boga, a Jan mu bylo na imie', in *Jan XXIII i jego dzielo. Praca zbioreowa*, ed. B.Bejze, B.Dziwosza and W.Ziólka, Warsaw 1972, 41–156.

27. Archivio Roncalli, Bologna, 52.35, f.13 ds.

28. Important research on the Tsar by A.Roccucci is in progress; furthermore a seminar was held in September 1996 on the participation of Central and Eastern Europe at Vatican II, convened in Lublin on the initiative of J.Kloczowski.

29. Cf. the testimony and documentation of V.Carbone, 'Schemi e discussioni sull'ateismo e sul marxismo nel Concilio Vaticano II. Documentazione', *Rivista di storia della chiesa in Italia* 44, 1990, 11–12.

30. Cf. D.Menozzi, 'L'anticoncilio', in *Il Vaticano II e la chiesa*, ed. G.Alberigo and J.P.Jossua, Brescia 1985.

31. For this see now the initiatives taken by Cardinal Siri, cf. B.Lai, *Il papa non eletto. Giuseppe Siri cardinale di Santa Romana Chiesa*, Rome and Bari 1993.

32. For the 'pessimistic' attitude of Congar, cf. my 'Parallelismi, nodi comuni e ipotesi conflittuali nelle strutture della preparazione del Vatican II', *in Verso il concilio Vaticano II (1960–1962)*, ed. G.Alberigo and A.Melloni, Genoa 1993, 482; the faith with which Chenu arrived at Vatican II was different – but singular – see M.-D.Chenu, *Notes quotidiennes au Concile*, ed A.Melloni, Paris 1995.

33. Already in 1963 an article appearing in *Réforme* argued that the telegram from Constantinople with which the Ecumenical Patriarch informed Moscow of the decision not to send observers to Rome had been blocked by the Communist Party.

34. Cf. a maximal picture in *Storia della Chiesa* XXV/1: *La Chiesa del Vaticano II* (1958–1978), ed. E.Guerriero, Milan 1994.

35. QO, STS, 11, 96 (conclave 1963): EU 30.24: tel Maregeri from Bonn, 27 May 1963.

36. A project of reconstructing diplomatic activities during Vatican II is now limited to the collection of sources in the archives of the foreign ministries of Rome, Paris, Bonn, London, Dublin, Lisbon, Madrid, Buenos Aires, Washington, Amman and Cairo; for the preparation cf. my 'Governi e diplomazie all'annuncio del Vaticano II', in *A la veille de Concile Vatican II. Vota et réactions en Europe et dans le Catholicisme oriental*, ed. M.Lamberigts and C.Soetens, Louvain 1992, 214–57.

The Ecumenical Problem in the Russian Orthodox Church in Relation to the 1994 Synod

Georgy Zyablitsev

I would like to begin this article with a personal recollection of three years ago. In September 1993 I was asked to be present as a representative of the Department for Foreign Relations of the Patriarchate of Moscow at the pastoral visit which the Primate of the Roman Catholic Church, Pope John Paul II, made in Lithuania, Latvia and Estonia. The Pope had occasion to meet both with Orthodox bishops of these countries and with me, and spoke to me, calling me '*ksjadz* (Polish Catholic priest) of Moscow'. After the mass near the 'Mount of Crosses' in Lithuania (a very well known place where by tradition people put crosses to commemorate important events in their lives), the Pope invited me to a meal in a small monastery. In the course of our conversation at table, among other things we touched on the question of conservative anti-ecumenical tendencies present in Russian Orthodoxy and the reasons for them.

I gave the Pope my opinion; in particular I said that one of the causes of the phenomenon was the inadequacy of theological training, due to the fact that up to the Gorbachev era the Russian church schools, which had been reopened after long closure at the end of the Second World War, had not been authorized by the atheistic power to admit students with higher education (there was even a precise secret order to this effect). We can see the sad fruits of this policy even today. The other aspect of the problem was the widespread use in these schools of outdated textbooks from pre-Revolutionary times which explained the problems of relations between the churches in the spirit of a bitter anti-Catholic polemic with a Byzantine character. State atheism did everything it could to transform the church into an archaeological museum: it was prohibited from engaging in any kind of social activities, theology was not developed in practice, and the whole of church life was essentially reduced to the liturgy. The 'protectionist' conservative tendencies were also a result of the opposition of believers to attempts made by the regime to destroy the religion, to the 'innovators'' schism of the 1920s *(obnovlenchestvo)*, and the cruel persecutions of the church in the 1930s and 1940s. In recent years the influx of missionaries from the West who have tried to fill the undeniable spiritual void created in Russia in the last seventy years has fed conservative tendencies. The proselytizing aspect that the activity of these missionaries (including also a few Catholics) assumes encourages anti-Protestant and anti-Catholic feelings among the Orthodox clergy, monks and laity. A harsh reaction has also been provoked among the Orthodox by the aggressive methods with which the Greek Catholics are renewing their ecclesiastical structures in West Ukraine.

I tried to explain all this to the Pope in the course of our conversation. He listened attentively and said that, despite all the difficulties, he had not lost hope in an improvement in relations between our churches. I replied with a famous phrase of Platon, Metropolitan of Moscow: 'Thank God, the barriers between the confessions do not reach to heaven.' 'What magnificent words!' said the Pope. 'Who spoke them? Platonov?' 'No,' I replied, 'they are the words of a Russian theologian of the nineteenth century, Metropolitan Platon.'

These recollections are meant to be a kind of preface to what I want to say. Between 29 November and 2 December 1994 the Synod of Bishops of the Russian Orthodox church was held in Moscow, and undoubtedly constituted an important event in our church life. The Synod had been preceded by the work of the Theological Commission at the Holy Synod, which had examined the problems connected with relations between our church and the other confessions, and those relating to our participation in the ecumenical movement. The result of the work of this commission was the report presented to the Synod by its president, Filaret, Metropolitan of Minsk and Slutsk. The particular attention given by the commission to such questions was anything but casual. September 1994 had seen the publication of an 'Open letter by the monks of the monastery of Valaam to His Holiness the Patriarch of Moscow and all Russia Aleksi II'. In it the monks of Valaam expressed the state of mind of many monks, priests and laity, and declared that they were 'profoundly grieved by the participation of Orthodox archbishops and bishops in the scandalous heretical ecumenical movement and in ecumenical prayer'. They asked that 'an end be put to ecumenical propaganda in the seminaries and theological academies' and that Orthodox should no longer take part 'in prayers and liturgies with heretics, pagans and Jews, whom the Lord already defined as a synagogue of Satan (Rev.3.9)', but 'should leave the World Council of Churches and, by means of a synod, excommunicate ecumenism as the heresy of all heresies'. Diodore, Patriarch of Jerusalem, known for his anti-ecumenical views, was hailed by them as the 'admiral of orthodoxy', while to their primate, His Holiness Patriarch Aleksi II, they said the following: 'When it pronounces words of edification, then we shall listen with veneration to the familiar voice of our pastor: but when You do not speak according to Christ, afflicted we shall turn our head, forgiving it with love and patience.' According to the words of the monks of Valaam, 'through ecumenism the freemasons want to embrace all the confessions, mixing truth with the lie', and, 'the aim of Satan is to destroy the church of Christ through the ecumenical movement, or more precisely to deprive it of grace'.

Shortly after the Synod, a small book was distributed, printed no one knows by whom, with a speech by Vitaly Archbishop of Montreal and Canada (of the Russian Church in Exile) given in the United States in 1967 at the Synod of Bishops of the Russian Church in Exile. In this speech, entitled 'Ecumenism', he says in particular that 'ecumenism is the heresy of heresies, since the ecumenical phenomenon includes all heresy in it... It is beyond doubt a phenomenon of apocalyptic character... The World Council of Churches is quite similar to the United Nations Organization. It can be supposed that the Antichrist will preside over both organizations, but that in spirit he will be closer to the World Council of Churches... Ecumenism aspires to demolish the frontiers of the Church of Christ. God exists and He exists in His one Holy, Catholic and Apostolic Church. However, all the other so-called Christian religions, monotheistic or pagan, all without even minimal exclusion – whether they are Catholicism, Protestantism, Islam or Buddhism – are obstacles placed by the devil between the Church of Christ and the human race.'

This speech on ecumenism (the passages quoted speak for themselves) could be acquired even in the bookshop of the Danilov Monastery in Moscow, where the synod was held. An 'Anti-Catholic Catechism' was also distributed, reprinted from a work dating from shortly before the Revolution, which in traditional Byzantine style accused the Catholic Church of 'heresy' and 'deviationism'; as was a book by a certain S.Nosov, *The Papacy and its Struggle against Orthodoxy*, full to the brim of false quotations from Vatican I and II. The book opens with a rhetorical question: 'What trust can we place in a Roman Catholic papism based on the lie and completely permeated with the lie, when it has not denied its pernicious lie decisively and publicly?' And it ends with these words: 'We do not dare to foresee future events; however, we can ask a question: is not perhaps the Pope the forerunner of the Antichrist who is to come?'

Among other anti-ecumenical publications, I should mention the declaration of the public committee 'For the Moral Rebirth of the Homeland', entitled *Ecumenism: A Way towards Depravation and Satanism*; it asserts that 'membership of the World Council of Churches stains the whole church and can become the object of the wrath of God'. Among the first publications of this kind, note needs to be taken of a book by two Bulgarian authors, Archimandrite Serafim and Archimandrite Sergei, a large edition of which was printed in Russia in 1992: *Why Christian Orthodoxy Cannot be Ecumenical*. This is a text which enjoys great authority in contemporary Russian monasticism. At the end we can read that 'our Orthodox consciousness does not allow us to be ecumenical, since this means serving Satan and his servant, the Antichrist'. According to the authors, ecumenism is pledged to the building up of a syncretistic pantheon of all the religions in which Orthodoxy, too, can find a welcome at the price of abandoning the idea of its own rightness and truth.

One of the Russian Orthodox authors best known for his anti- ecumenical, anti-Catholic and anti-Protestant positions in recent years has been Ioann, the Metropolitan of St Petersburg and Ladoga.[1] Many books and articles on these themes have been published in his name or edited by him; given the enormous quantity, I shall not attempt to discuss them here. All these and many other anti-ecumenical publications produced a quite particular atmosphere in the Russian Orthodox Church on the eve of the Synod.

On 15 and 16 November, with the Synod now about to happen, the Danilov Monastery in Moscow held a conference on 'The Unity of the Church', organized by the Theological Institute of St Tikhon and the Theological Academy of Moscow, in which representatives of other theological schools, monks and some bishops took part. The conference had three basic themes: nationalism and the church; the schisms in the church, their nature and their role in contemporary church life; and the traditions and the reforms in the life of the church,. The term 'neo- innovatorism' (*neoobnovlenchestvo*) often cropped up during the course of the conference; two Moscow priests, Georgy Kochetkov and Aleksandr Borisov, were regarded as the main exponents of this 'heresy'. They were accused of 'modernism', 'reformism' and 'sectarianism', Russification of the cult (i.e. the use of some texts in Russian and not in Old Slavonic), and circulating Protestant and Catholic literature in their parishes, propagating the doctrine that the mystical frontiers of the Church are wider than its canonical frontiers (according to Kochetkov, Mahatma Gandhi, too, is included in this 'mystical church'), and Islam, Buddhism and Taoism are also religions revealed by God. Kochetkov was also criticized for having reintroduced the ancient practice of the agape, with the breaking of bread and the distribution of bread and wine as a parody of the eucharist, and Borisov for his book *Whitened Fields*, in which speakers at the conference found a large number of deviations from Orthodox doctrine. The tenor of the conference was well expressed by the words of a professor from the Theological Academy of Moscow, Archimandrite Platon: 'Conservatism is a very fine word: it means that the church must be identical to itself.'

Despite the length and tone of some of the speeches at the conference, the final document did not issue any anathema. This prompted the monks of Valaam to publish a new furious document against the 'heresy of neo-innovatorism' and ecumenism which stated, among other things: 'Today, at the end of time, the heresy of all heresies has sprung into action: universal neo-innovatorism. Its fulcrum is ecumenism. The plan of the heretics is simple: on the pretext of uniting with them all those who say that they believe in God and unifying all of humanity, they seek to draw Holy Orthodoxy on to the tempestuous waves of the sea of universal heresy and to sink it.' The letter goes on to divide ecumenism into extreme and moderate ecumenism. The doctrine of 'extreme ecumenism' is described like this: 'The church of Christ, which is said to be divided into a multitude of heterodox churches, must be unified again, and therefore needs to seek unification with the heterodox, who like us worship the same God. In fact this denies the existence today of the one true Church of Christ on earth'.

There is then an illustration of 'moderate ecumenism', which accepts 'the existence of the One Church of Christ and the true faith beyond the confines of the Church'. This 'moderate ecumenism', according to the monks of Valaam, is the fulcrum of 'neo-innovatorism'; in support of this opinion they quote a passage from a lecture by Fr Georgy Kochetkov: 'To the degree to which the faith is present outside the church... a task arises, understood in a new way: to arrive at the unity of faith.' In this quotation the monks of Valaam detect a 'manifest heresy' and in particular 'the affirmation of the existence of the true faith outside the Church'. The letter also accuses 'certain Orthodox metropolitans' of a 'stubborn refusal to condemn ecumenism as the heresy of all heresies'. Evidently the monks placed such a hope above all in the Synod of Bishops of the Russian Orthodox Church, which at last we can discuss. First of all, however, I shall make some reference to the work of the theological commission within which the ecumenical problem was discussed on the eve of the Synod.

The Theological Commission at the Holy Synod had been instituted in 1994, and had made the ecumenical problem the centre of its attention. In the first place the Commission had to provide an evaluation of the joint document subscribed to at Chambesy in 1990 by some Orthodox Churches and by the Pre-Chalcedonian Eastern Churches (Monophysites). The document had been produced using the peculiar terminology of St Cyril of Alexandria, venerated both by the Orthodox and the Monophysites. However, the main difficulty lies in the fact that there is no open recognition in the document from the Monophysite side of the ecumenical councils after the third, and the christological differences were redefined after the Council of Ephesus. One of the members of the commission put it like this: 'If we signed this document I fear that we would incur the excommunication of all the ecumenical councils after the fourth.' In his report to the Synod on this topic the president of the Theological Commission, Metropolitan Filaret, expressed the conviction of the Commission that it could not accept the joint document of Chambesy as definitive.

During the sessions of the Theological Commission there was particularly lively discussion of the question of the participation of the Russian Orthodox Church in ecumenical organizations. There were extremist calls to leave all ecumenical organizations, first of all the World Council of Churches, the Conference of European Churches and the Ecumenical Council of European Youth; motions were put to move from member status to observer status. Those who argued for this point of view primarily based their position on the fact, first, that the influence of ecumenism would tend to uproot the dogmatic truth from its foundation, and secondly, that all this, in particular ecumenical prayers with the heterodox, would scandalize believers. That such disorientation and sense of scandal were in fact present among the faithful is clearly attested by the publications and the books which I mentioned above. Those who argued for the continuation of our participation in the ecumenical movement pointed out that our break with ecumenism would be transformed into a break with Orthodoxy in its fullness, given that some Orthodox churches are not only part of the ecumenical movement but are even to be numbered among the founders of ecumenical organizations. In any case, the question would have to be discussed in a pan-Orthodox assembly. Compromise positions were also put forward: to leave ecumenical organizations while maintaining good and fraternal contacts with the heterodox, in particular in the sphere of social activities and diaconia. The archpriest Vitaly Borovoi, already a representative of the Russian Orthodox Church at the World Council of Churches, showed in his speech how our church had established ecumenical contacts a short time before the Revolution, and could even say that it was among the sources of the Faith and Order Movement. In particular, in 1917 Patriarch Tikhon sent a letter with his blessing to the president of Faith and Order in the name of the Moscow Synod of that year, and supported the initiative of the Week of Prayer for Christian Unity. Even before that, in the nineteenth century, the Russian Orthodox Church had promoted a very intense and fruitful dialogue with the Anglicans. In general the Russian Orthodox Church took an active part in the ecumenical movement until 1927, when that became impossible as a result of its forced isolation from international relations. Our representatives were able to take part in the meeting organized by Faith and Order at Geneva in 1920, and at the World Conference of Lausanne in 1927; after this date, only the Russian theologians of the Institute of St Sergius in Paris took part in ecumenical conferences. All these facts were recalled in Metropolitan Filaret's speech to the Synod, entitled 'Relations with the Other Confessions and the Participation of the Orthodox Church in the Ecumenical Movement'.

In his speech to the synod, Metropolitan Filaret first of all stated that we had to refuse the invitation to the First General Assembly of the World Council of Churches in 1948 because 'of the grave emergency in our situation at the time', in short, because of the pressure of the atheistic regime; it had been absolutely necessary for us to become members of this organization in 1961, given Kruschchev's new persecution of the church. This was 'useful and indispensable for our church and its faithful'. Metropolitan Filaret then mentioned the 'results' of the Orthodox participation in the World Council of Churches and its testimony to it, above all the New Delhi resolution of 1961 on unity and the Toronto Declaration of 1950 which guaranteed the full independence and inviolability of the position and convictions of the Orthodox Church. The 1982 Lima resolution on Baptism, Eucharist and Ministry and the results of the Fifth World Conference at Santiago di Compostella in 1993 were also highly valued by the Orthodox.

Metropolitan Filaret also went on to note the negative tendencies in the development of the World Council of Churches, a cause of disquiet among the Orthodox. First of all there was 'unlimited ecumenism', or the tendency to express the interests of all the Christian groups and movements, including the feminist and youth movements, the religious and cultural movements and so on. In the specific conditions of this tendency, the unity of faith was as it were relegated to second place. Secondly, there was the attempt by some of the members to transform the ecumenical movement of the Christian churches into an inter-religious movement including Muslims, Buddhists and Jews, which carried with it the risk of syncretism and eclecticism and destroyed the understanding that salvation could be achieved only through the church of Christ. The practice of 'eucharistic hospitality' also created the illusion that the degree of unity in the faith already achieved could be sufficient. In his letter to the conference at Santiago di Compostella, His Holiness Patriarch Aleksi stated clearly that a partial unity was insufficient for full *koinonia* and that communion could be established only after complete unity of faith had been achieved on the basis of the doctrine of the early church.

The speech also discussed the proselytization by Western missionaries (moreover, it was emphasized that the World Council itself condemned proselytism). Severe words were also directed against the 'proselytizing activity of the Catholic Church and the aggressive attitude of the Uniate Churches', emphasizing how missionary activity tinged with proselytism 'compromises the understanding of the very idea of ecumenical community and common witness with the Protestants and the idea of "sister churches" previously welcomed in Catholic-Orthodox dialogue for the re-establishment of communion, and finally even the sense of pursuing such a dialogue with the Catholic Church'.

The last point in Metropolitan Filaret's speech was devoted to the problem of ecumenical prayers. Again in the course of the sessions of the Theological Commission it had been said that such prayer incurred the excommunication provided for by fourth and fifth century canons on 'prayers with heretics'. It was said that prayer with the heterodox corrupted the Orthodox flock, in particular the honours reserved in the churches for heterodox hierarchs, which would denote a recognition of the 'sacramental and canonical legitimacy of their ordination'. The speaker emphasized how for the Orthodox the idea and practice of prayer for Christian unity was a way of testifying to their own faith before Western Christians: there was no text in this prayer which was not Orthodox. As for the accusation that ecumenical prayer was 'prayer with the heretics', the Orthodox Church had never declared in council that the Catholics or the Protestants or the Anglicans were heretics. In general the problem relating to ecumenical prayer was left to diocesan bishops; in any case they had to try not to give occasion for scandal to believers. And with this Metropolitan Filaret's speech ended.

In evaluating the significance of this speech, which was the basis for one of the resolutions of the Synod, it can be noted that the head of the Russian Orthodox Church rejected the extreme anti-ecumenical views with precise arguments, again pointing out that our participation in the ecumenical movement was first of all dictated by motives of ecclesiastical usefulness, but at the same time with full sincerity bringing out the negative tendencies – from an Orthodox perspective – of the ecumenical movement. However, that did not necessarily entail a departure from ecumenical organizations; on the contrary, as His Holiness Patriarch Aleksi had said in his speech to the Holy Synod, 'the time has also come for our church to help the ecumenical movement to retain those elements of pan-Orthodox testimony which were welcomed by the ecumene and which could be lost if we deprived it of our testimony, in a situation of the crisis for Western civilization, when secularization is being reinforced, destroying the spiritual foundations of man and preventing him from turning to God... Therefore, being actively involved in collaboration between Christians, in recent decades the Russian Orthodox Church has maintained bilateral relations with the Roman Catholic church, the Churches of the Anglican Communion, the Old Catholic Churches, the Evanglical Lutheran Churches and churches and communities of different confessions.'

I would like to conclude with more words of His Holiness Patriarch Aleksi II, in his 1994–1995 Christmas message to listeners on Vatican Radio:

> The spiritual strengths of Christians take on particular significance as the end of the second millennium of the Church of Christ approaches. In truth this great jubilee which is now so very near requires Christians to renew the whole system of spiritual life, to strengthen faith and testimony and to renew zeal for all good works, for justice, faith, charity and peace (II Tim.2.22). The new forces of the church directed towards the restoration of Christian unity and a renewed frankness in interconfessional dialogue are also important. In particular, the mystical unity of the Church as the body of Christ must prompt Christians, on the threshold of the great jubilee, to overcome divisions and schism, to exclude all forms of proselytism, and to collaborate fraternally for the glory of God.

Notes

1. Metropolitan Ioann (Snytsev) of St Petersburg and Ladoga died on 2 November 1995; on 26 December the Holy Synod in ordinary succession, presided over by Aleksi II, Patriarch of Moscow, nominated Metropolitan Vladimir (Kotlyarov) to the cathedra of St Petersburg.

Eastern Catholic Churches and Uniatism

Étienne Fouilloux

'At the request of the Orthodox Church the normal progress of theological dialogue with the Catholic Church has been interrupted so that the question known as "Uniatism" may immediately be touched on. On the method which has been called "Uniatism" it was stated at Freising (in June 1990) that "we reject this as a method of seeking unity because it is opposed to the common tradition of our churches". As far as the Eastern Catholic Churches are concerned, it is clear that as part of the Catholic Communion they have the right to exist and to act in response to the spiritual needs of their faithful.' This solemn declaration by the International Commission for Theological Dialogue between the Catholic Church and the Orthodox Church which met at Balamand (Lebanon) between 17 and 24 June 1993 would seem unequivocal.[1] However, what 'Uniatism' is still needs to be specified, and that would seem to be difficult.

In fact 'Uniatism' is a term with highly polemical connotations. Until relatively recently it was used almost exclusively by the Eastern churches and Christians separated from Rome to denote a kind of toning down of the schism which was unacceptable in their eyes, and also its specific results: Catholic communities with an Eastern rite which had originated from their mother churches, often through painful schism.[2] Like Catholicism as a whole, those mainly concerned have long preferred a more neutral designation: 'Unionism' for the method and 'United Churches' or 'Eastern rite' for its result.[3] But whether called Uniatism or Unionism, Uniates or United, the entity and the people certainly exist at the end of the twentieth century, and the announcement of their death or the regaining of their vitality continues to trouble interconfessional understanding to the point of requiring a declaration like that of Balamand. That is one more reason for the historian to investigate their origins and their evolution, which is now arousing an interest in the West equal to the former ignorance.[4]

The history of the Christian communities united with Rome who have kept their rite comprises at least two major phases. Until the second half of the nineteenth century, various fragments of the Christian East wished for such a union, but in such different regions, at such different times and in such different forms that it seems impossible to link them by a continuous thread. For strictly circumstantial and local reasons, where political motives (in the broader sense) were competing with strictly religious motives, these unions were produced without clearly having been, from the side of Rome, the fruit of any overall strategy other than the constant but vague desire to put an end to the great schism between East and West. Thus it is that the Christian populations who took refuge on Mount Lebanon as a result of the Arab conquest and derive themselves from the old Monk Maron have found themselves in communion with the see of Peter since the beginning of the thirteenth century without any break in continuity. At the end of the sixteenth century, the Ruthenians of the great Polish-Lithuanian state which formed a kind of advanced bastion of Latin Catholicity facing the Orthodox East decided to become reconciled with Rome: this was the Union of Brest, the fourth centenary of which is being celebrated this year, in 1996. A century later, the populations of Transylvania rescued from Turkish rule by the Habsburgs also made a union (Alba Julia, 1698); however, they only obtained a hierarchy of their own in the middle of the nineteenth century. At the beginning of the eighteenth century, Christians of the Patriarchate of Antioch attached themselves to Rome without abandoning their rite, to form the Melkite Catholic church. The distance between places, times and situations is enough to prove the absence of any connection between these various alliances.

Furthermore, the communities which arose from them have had a difficult life. They were in fact immediately and vigorously challenged by their mother churches who bluntly accused them of treason. The clearest case here is that of the Ruthenians: in 1623 Josaphat Kuncewicz, the United Archbishop of Polotsk, was put to death by his compatriots who remained faithful to Orthodoxy (he was canonized by Rome three centuries later). And one cannot say that in return they received solid support from their new fellow religionists. For both nationalistic and religious reasons the Latin Poles, for example, considered the United Ruthenians to be second-order Catholics, the Latinization (and Polonization...) of whom was a major pastoral objective. Generally speaking, in a massively Latin Catholic Church the Eastern rites are too weak to constitute a credible alternative: their progressive Latinization would appear inevitable; and Latinization only confirms the Orthodox suspicions towards them: their liturgical autonomy becomes a veneer which will not long resist Roman centralization. In these conditions it seems very difficult to be fully Catholic and fully Eastern. Considered as false Easterners by the Orthodox and second-order Catholics by the Latins, the faithful of these churches, however ancient and deep their roots, find it difficult to preserve their own personality. The scant attention paid to their opposition to the definition of papal infallibility by Vatican I in 1870 shows the weakness of their credit in Rome, even if Pius IX did not interfere with the Melkite patriarch Gregory Yussef, as a pious legend would have it.[5]

However, a significant change in the Roman attitude towards these United communities came under the pontificate of Leo XIII (1878–1903). In 1862, an Eastern section responsible for their affairs had already been created within the Roman congregation *De Propaganda Fide*. This was the beginning of the idea that the Christian East can in no way be likened to a mission field. But it was not until the next pontificate, and the expected disintegration of the Ottoman Empire, that the Vatican disposition towards the United communities modified substantially, in the texts if not always on the ground. After an International Eucharistic Congress held at Jerusalem in 1893, the encyclical *Orientalium dignitas* sensitively revalued the role of the churches of the Eastern rite within Catholicism (1894). Followed by a long series of related measures, it began the substitution of a 'Unionist' strategy for a 'missionary' strategy, first at Rome and then on the ground. What did this involve? It was no longer necessary to convert individually Christians separated from Latin Catholicism, an activity in which a number of Western religious families were engaged. On the contrary, it was necessary to reinforce the United communities by scrupulously respecting their usages and customs, particularly in the field of liturgy. In other words there was a braking, and if possible a reversal, of the secular movement of Latinization that was eating away at them. For they were the living proof of the catholicity of a church which did not want to present itself as exclusively Latin. Provided, of course, that they had local credibility, they too were a bridge with those who at that time were called 'dissidents' and the matrix of their ultimate return as a body to the Petrine fold. That, at least, was the opinion which prevailed in certain Vatican circles at the end of the nineteenth century, though not without internal conflicts.

After a missionary renewal under the pontificate of Pius X (1903–1914), this strategy became institutionalized under his successor Benedict XV at the very moment (and this is no coincidence!) when the First World War dislocated not only the Ottoman empire but also the Russian empire: the collapse of these monarchies with strong religious connotations seemed to promise bright new dawns for Eastern Catholicism. So in 1917 a Roman dicastery fully concerned with the East was finally separated from the Propaganda: the Congregation for the Eastern Churches. It was also in 1917 that the Pontifical Eastern Institute, charged with securing clergy of quality for these churches, was founded. One can say that such a 'Unionist' strategy which put the concern for a return of the East to Rome in the hands of the United churches was practised by the Vatican, with many ups and downs, until the beginning of the 1960s. Despite the failure of the Russian mirage of the inter-war period, the liquidation of the United communities in Sovietized Europe after 1945 and the growing pressure of the Muslim challenge to the Near East, the concern to support these suffering churches did not weaken during the pontificates of Pius XI and Pius XII. As proof of this we can see the growing authority of the Eastern Congregation under the aegis of the French Cardinal Tisserant (1936–1959) or the important work of the purification of liturgical books and the formation of a specific code of canon law. The process of Latinization seemed to have been checked; and Rome made great effort to help its Eastern Christians... while keeping a close eye on them.[6]

Viewed from the end of the twentieth century, the fruits of such a long and complex development seem very varied. In fact Catholicism of the Eastern rite is made up of two groups which are very different both in antiquity and in their respective importance. The churches that history over the centuries has brought near to Rome in one way or another are by far the best implanted and the most powerful: the Ukrainian Church, the Romanian church of Transylvania, the Maronite Church of Lebanon and the Melkite Church of the Near East, to which must be added the Malabar Church of Kerala, in South India. At the time of its elimination in 1946, the former alone numbered more than 40% of the some ten to eleven million United Christians; and the five communities amounted to more than 80% of the same total.[7]

If these churches have undergone decades or centuries of hostility, not to mention persecution, from their Orthodox compatriots, and centuries of Latinization or centralization on the part of Rome, it is because there is nothing artificial about them. Whether one deplores them or rejoices at them, they incarnate a certain kind of religious adhesion, the same Eastern and Catholic movement. However they are also, and perhaps above all, a powerful factor of national, regional or local identification. The Maronite Church has played this role for the mountain people of Lebanon in their Muslim environment, as the Ukrainian Church has for the peasants of

Eastern Galicia resistant to all Russification, or the union of Alba Julia for those people in Transylvania who were belatedly annexed to a greater Romania with an Orthodox majority. We can easily see how such political and religious particularisms have been able to present, and continue to present, problems of cohesion to the states which at one time or another have included them in their frontiers, for example greater Poland between the two wars for the Ukrainians; and Lebanon, which has been statutorily multi-confessional since the 1943 pact, for the Maronites. But there is no justified reason, whether political, religious or a mixture of the two, to block these ancient communities, numerous and well-implanted. This is precisely what the Balamand Declaration says. Like it, we suggest keeping for them the title of Eastern Catholic Churches and thus banishing from them any understanding in terms of 'Uniatism'.

On the other hand, the 'Unionist' strategy of 1890–1960 gave birth in quite an artificial form to small United communities in countries with an overwhelming Orthodox majority. Thus we can list, without being exhaustive, the creation (or recreation) of a hierarchy of the Eastern rite: in Coptic Egypt in 1899;[8] in the kingdom of Greece in 1911; in Revolutionary Russia in 1917; or in conquered Bulgaria in 1926. Simply from the point of view of effectiveness, before any basic appreciation, we must note the failure of such attempts, which sought to transform a series of case studies into a quasi-universal model for the return of the East to Roman unity. Scanty flocks of faithful directed by a few pastors (whose intentions are not in question), these communities, far from winning over a significant part of their compatriots, remained very much a minority among them. Numbering seventeen, they represented less than 20% of the faithful depending on the Eastern Congregation in 1962.[9]

However, their symbolic importance far surpasses their real importance: instead of convincing, they serve to hinder encounter with Rome and also provide an excuse for the notorious reluctance of vast sectors of Orthodoxy to engage in ecumenical dialogue. The Greek and Romanian cases are the most testing here. Do they not in fact seem to be proof of the duality of the Vatican apparatus: eirenical at the summit and proselytizing at the grass roots? If the Balamand Declaration has any meaning, it is that it breaks with the voluntarism which consisted in creating United communities throughout the countries of the East, sometimes out of nothing. So I propose to reserve the term 'Uniatism' for this voluntarism and its meagre results.[10]

But why are the Eastern Christians united to Rome so prominent an element in the religious chronicle today? The hostility towards them on the part of an Orthodoxy which has always considered them at best as the victims of a fraud and at worst as the agents of an unworthy seduction has been unrelenting. Moreover this hostility emphasizes the congenital malformation of 'Unionism': this claimed remedy for disunion is judged worse than the evil. In fact the wound which has never healed has been reopened by the telescoping in the course of the last three decades of two quite unexpected phenomena: on the one hand the official move of the Roman Church towards the ecumenical movement, which was of no importance to it previously, and on the other the recognition of the United churches in Eastern Europe.

John XXIII's main objective for his Council, the rapprochement of separated Christians, took a giant step there. Vatican II even saw the previous Unionist line replaced by an ecumenical one. This was a substitution in the strict sense of the term, since the schema on union prepared by the Eastern Commission (i.e. the Eastern Congregation) was withdrawn at the first session (1962) and replaced by a text from the Secretariat for Christian Unity which in 1964 became the conciliar decree *Unitatis redintegratio*. This document records the main contributions of the ecumenical movement, both outside Catholicism and within, over half a century: a global vision of the unity desired, without any privilege, for the East; an exclusively spiritual approach to the problem, in other words one stripped of any spirit of short- or medium-term conquest.

But is the substitution complete? It would be a misunderstanding of the Roman Church's mistrust of the brutal changes to believe this. On 21 November 1964, just as the decree on ecumenism was being promulgated by Paul VI, a decree on the Eastern Catholic Churches appeared from the Eastern Commission with quite a different tone. Completely in line with 'Unionism', it calls for the reinforcement of the United communities, which still have an important role to play on the chessboard of interconfessional relations. It is only one step from there to believe that Rome is keeping two irons in the fire, and this step is sometimes taken in the East. If the Western church and the Eastern churches which are separated from it are sister churches, as Paul VI was not afraid of stating, what can be the justification for the support by Rome of churches separated from their sister churches at Lvov, Alba Julia or Damascus? Until the end of the 1970s, the power of the ecumenical wave was such that these questions hardly arose. Nevertheless, they contributed to delaying the opening of a real theological dialogue between East and West while irritating the United churches, sorely tested by some among them who did not hide their fears of being sacrificed to the gains and losses of the ecumenical cause.[11]

*

However, the problem has become burningly topical since the election of a Slavonic Pope to the chair of Peter in 1978 and the resurrection of the United churches freed from the Communist yoke a decade later, while the Islamic offensive has been mounting in the Middle East. Particularly in Ukraine and in Romania, martyr churches then emerged from the catacombs; they called for the consideration and the property of which they had been deprived forty years earlier for the benefit of Orthodoxy, and local tension became very great. Moreover, the Orthodox authorities were tempted to subordinate the prolongation of ecumenical dialogue to a clear choice of Rome between what seemed to them to be incompatible lines: ecumenism and Unionism, which they uniformly call Uniatism.

Balamand, and also John Paul II, have given us a twofold response: there is no question of going back on the way of complete unity, as is shown by the encyclical *Ut Unum sint*; nor is there any question of sacrificing the United churches at the same time as Uniatism, as was shown by the pontifical letter to the Ukrainians and Ruthenians for the fourth centenary of the Union of Brest, some weeks previously.[12] In theory things are clear, but in practice? How can we not see different hands, and thus different influences, extending right to the heart of the Roman Curia, in the two texts cited? And how can we distinguish in practice between guilty proselytism and the legitimate apostolate of a no less legitimate church? Balamand has clarified the debate, as I have tried to do here. But clarification does not mean extinction. From a human perspective, for a long time still the United churches will remain a subject of friction between Catholicism, which cannot and will not sacrifice them to a hypothetical reconciliation between East and West, and an Orthodoxy which feels the greatest difficulty in accepting the very principle of their existence, as is shown by all its history, ancient and more recent.[13]

Notes

1. The complete text of the declaration can be found in *Istina* 4, 1993, 387–93: 387.
2. See for example the recent short synthesis by Jean-Claude Roberti, *Les Uniates*, Paris 1992.
3. There are clear reservations on the part of Cardinal Tisserant, secretary of the Congregation for Eastern Churches, 11 March 1939, *Istina* (n.1), 402–3. Against this, see Joseph Hajjar, *Les chrétiens uniates du Proche-Orient*, Paris 1962 (however, the author belongs to a United church, the Melkite church).
4. As is witnessed, for France, by the well-deserved success of the book by Jean-Pierre Valognes, *Vie et mort des chrétiens d'Orient des origines à nos jours*, Paris 1995.
5. Constantin G.Patelos, *Vatican I et les évêques uniates. Une étape éclairante de la politique romaine a l'égard des Orientaux (1867–1870)*, Louvain 1981.

6. There are recent syntheses on the contemporary history of the Christian East in *Histoire du christianisme, 11, Libéralisme, industrialisation, expansion européenne (1830–1914)*: 'Christianisme et nationalité dans l'Europe du Centre-Est' (Jerzy Kloczowski, 703–29); 'L'Église orthodoxe russe de la fin du XIXe au debut du XXe siècle: isolement et intégration' (Constantin Simon, 733–92); 'Les chrétiens d'Orient au XIXe siècle: un renouveau lourd de menaces' (Catherine Mayeur-Jaouen, 793–849), Paris 1995; *12, Guerres mondiales et totalitarismes (1914–1958)*: 'Les chrétiens d'Orient menacés' (Étienne Fouilloux, 743–831), Paris 1990. There is a bibliography prior to 1990 on the history of Roman 'Unionism' in Étienne Fouilloux, *Au coeur du XXe siècle religieux*, Paris 1993 (Part Two, 'Cet Orient méconnu', 115–201). The most important of recent publications include: Angelo Tamborra, *Studi storici sull'Europa orientale*, Rome 1986; Gisueppe M.Croce, *La badia greca di Grottaferrata e la Rivista 'Roma e l'Oriente'*, Vatican 1990; Léon Tretjakewitsch, *Bishop Michel d'Herbigny SJ and Russia*, Würzburg 1990; Roberto Morozzo della Rocca, *'Le nazioni non muiono'. Russia rivoluzionaria, Polonia independete e Santa Sede*, Bologna 1992; Andrea Riccardi, *Il Vaticano e Mosca 1940–1990*, Bari 1992; Vittorio Peri, *Orientalis varietas. Rome e le Chiese d'Oriente*, Rome 1994.

7. Estimates made on the basis of very precise figures (but how were they collected?) provided by the Eastern Congregation, *Oriente cattolico. Cenni storici e statistiche*, Vatican City 1962.

8. A recent case studied by Claude Soetens, 'Origine et developpement de l'Église copte catholique', *Irénikon* 1992, 42–62.

9. Still the Copts, Ethiopians, Malankars, Syrians, Albanians, Balts, Byelorussians, Bulgarians, Chinese, Finns, Georgians, Greeks, Italo-Albanians, Japanese, Russians Yugoslavs and Armenians.

10. The multiplication of popular works does not make up for the absence of a rigorous synthesis on the situation of Eastern Catholicism today. For the Middle East see the contribution by Giuseppe M.Croce to *Storia della Chiesa*, XXV/2, *La Chiesa del Vaticano II (1958–1978)*, Milan 1994, 579–607 (very up-to-date bibliography).

11. For the shift at the Council and the situation afterwards see my summaries, 'Au coeur du XXe siècle religieuse', 71–97, and *La Chiesa del Vaticano II (1958–1978)* (n.10), 249–7.

12. 25 May and 25 March respectively.

13. For a contradictory theological appreciation of the United churches and Uniatism see in particular *Irénikon* 3, 1992.

The Measures taken by the Moscow Patriarchate between 1990 and 1992 to settle the Interconfessional Conflict in West Ukraine

Georgy Zyablitsev

The religious and political situation in West Ukraine intensified especially after summer 1988. The Greek Catholic Christians, who had lived there illegally since 1946, ceased to be illegal and organized a massive anti-Orthodox propaganda campaign; they made themselves felt in Moscow and the Ukraine (by demonstrations, meetings, hunger strikes and open-air worship) and called for the restoration of the Union in the territories of West Ukraine. The beginning of active attacks by the Greek Catholicon on the Orthodox Church was the confiscation of the Cathedral of the Transfiguration, the second largest Orthodox church in L'viv, on the night of 29 October 1989. After that, in the space of a few month there was an avalanche of plundering of the communities of the Orthodox Church in the West Ukraine by Uniates.

The situation of the supporters of the Orthodox Church became extremely complicated in Spring 1990 when the representatives of the Ruch were victorious in March in the elections of local administrations in the areas of L'viv, Ivano-Frankivsk and Ternopil, and the newly-elected councils often quite openly supported the Uniate churches.

The climax of the catastrophic events for the Orthodox Church in West Ukraine was the occupation of St George Cathedral in L'viv by the Greek Catholics in August 1990. Bishop Andrei (Horak), who was present in the church at this time, was insulted, and for some months many Orthodox were refused normal conditions for the celebration of worship. The result of the situation described was an almost complete annihilation of three

Orthodox dioceses up to winter 1990/1991. In summer 1989 the diocese of L'viv had around 12,000 communities, while at the beginning of 1991 there were no more than 50 or 60. By spring 1991, the number of churches in the diocese of Ivano-Frankivsk, which formerly amounted to around 600, was reduced to no more than 25 to 30. In Ivano-Frankivsk and Ternopil the Orthodox hierarchs were kept out of the church buildings and worship was celebrated in small rooms which had been converted for the purpose at short notice. In connection with these events the Moscow Patriarchate initiated conversations with the Holy See to normalize the situation. The conversations took place in Moscow between 12 and 17 January 1990.

The communiqué of this meeting stated:

> In expressing their concern over the situation in West Ukraine, the representatives of the two churches noted that the problems of inter-church relations in this area are not caused by religion and expressly declare[1] that enmity and violence are not compatible with the Christian spirit.

Thus both sides recognized that after 1989 the question of the Uniates was being presented primarily as a political question, while the confessional differences were really secondary.

The protectors of the Union, especially in the Ruch and the 'left-wing' parties, assigned roles clearly: the Greek Catholic Church was the 'martyr church', the spiritual nucleus of the resistance against the 'Bolshevik occupation'; the rebirth of the Union was regarded as an element in the democratization of public life in the Ukraine.

By contrast, the Orthodox Church was seen as an official organization which served the Communists. Here the national factor also played an important role. In actively basing themselves on the authentically national character of Greek Catholicism, the theoreticians of 'the rebirth of the Union' exploited the powerful patriotic movement whihc had begun in the Ukraine in the years of perestroika; here of course they declared Orthodoxy to be the opponent of the free development of the Ukrainian people: it was branded 'Moscow faith' and a means of Russification. The nub of this problem was the question of liturgical language. Although Old Slavonic was the traditional language of worship in the Ukraine, worship in Ukrainian was a powerful instrument in the service of the popularity of Greek Catholicism.

The most important result of the meeting in January 1990 was the 'Recommendations for the Normalization of Relations between Orthodox and Catholics of the Eastern rite'.[2] This comprised twelve points:

1. Both sides confirm the loyalty of their churches to the principles of religious freedom and recognize that in the constitutional state these principles should be implemented for all on the basis of the law without any discrimination; they regard the fastest possible normalization of the situation of the Catholics of the Eastern rite in West Ukraine as a necessity.

2. This normalization is to open a new chapter in the history of relations between Catholics and Orthodox in this region: the opposition and injustice on both sides in the past is to be overcome in the spirit of true forgiveness and reconciliation, and that should lead to collaboration and to mutual testimony to Jesus Christ; for the church was called to preach this.

3. This normalization, which is being realized in the context of the general democratic transformation of the country, is to guarantee the Catholics of the Eastern rite the universal right to religious activity in accord with the constitution and laws of the USSR.

This right is not to be implemented without taking account of the rights and legitimate interests of the Orthodox and other religious groups.

We believe that the Christians of the USSR should contribute to the joint efforts leading to the creation of a just constitutional state.

4. In this connection it is very important to abandon all illegitimate actions, especially those which are accompanied by force. Such actions are incompatible with the Christian spirit and should be condemned; moreover they are a hindrance to the registration of the communities of the Catholics of the Eastern rite.

5. Here both sides note that the Catholic communities of the Eastern rite have a right and a possibility to be legally registered.

6. The Catholic communities which are registered in this way, like the communities of other confessions, have the right to maintain a place of worship for use free of charge and for an unlimited period, and also to build new churches or lease or buy property.

7. In noting the fact that communities have occasionally separated and each group – Orthodox and Catholic – equally claims exclusive use of the church building, we call on both to resolve the competing claims without enmity, in brotherly accord and recognition of the free election, without any pressure and on a legal basis.

8. The need to form a joint commission with the participation of representatives of the Holy See, the Moscow Patriarchate and the Orthodox and Catholics of West Ukraine for the resolution of practical questions which arise in the process of normalization between Orthodox and Catholics of the Eastern rite is unanimously recognized. Each of these groups is to be represented by one or a maximum of two members. The commission is to respect this agreement and resolve disputed questions in

the spirit of Christian love and brotherly co-operation. It is necessary to regulate as quickly as possible the situation in the churches which are occupied by Catholics of the Eastern rite without the consent of the above-mentioned communities. This regulation should be achieved in accord with the law, even before the registration of Catholic communities.

9. The community of Catholics of the Eastern rite came into being 400 years ago as an attempt to overcome the separation between the Orthodox and the Catholic Church. This attempt failed. For centuries the divisions which formed the sources of conflicts and suffering for Orthodox and Catholics remained.

In remaining true to Christ's commandment 'that they may all be one' and striving to keep this commandment in their relationships the two churches have entered on the new way of dialogue, since they are deeply convinced that they will be helped to resolve the problems which separate them. not by the methods of Union which have been practised in the past, but by dialogue. Such a dialogue has become possible thanks to the new approach to questions of Christian unity which have been worked out by the Second Vatican Council and a number of pan-Orthodox conversations.

The Eastern Catholic churches which came into being as a result of the Union of past centuries and have become a part of the Catholic Church are related to the Orthodox on the basis of the principles of the Second Vatican Council, and that gives them the opportunity to be a constructive element in Orthodox-Catholic relations.

Both sides are firmly convinced that today, and also in the future, these relations should be free from any proselytism and mutual suspicion, since the two churches can successfully progress on the way of dialogue only in an atmosphere of trust and collaboration.

10. In the continuation and development of efforts in the direction of unity, the question of the organization of the hierarchical structure of the Catholics of the Eastern rite in West Ukraine should be discussed, so that the impression does not arise that one hierarchy is opposed to another; here efforts should be made to fulfil the shared obligations which arise from the dialogue between our churches and the new form of brotherly relations which has arisen between us.

11. The two delegations will immediately pass on the recommendations mentioned above to their church authorities as they have been accepted in complete harmony. These recommendations remain confidential until their confirmation, and will be published immediately after they have been confirmed. We hope that the Catholics and Orthodox, united in the new spirit which is showing itself here, will continue their efforts for the normalization of the process which, we hope, will lead to the complete

settlement of the situation and contribute to the deepening of communion between Catholics and Orthodox. And this is happening to the praise of God.

On the basis of these recommendations a commission was formed with the participation of representatives of the Holy See, the Moscow Patriarchate, and the Ukrainian Orthodox and Greek Catholic Church. It worked in L'viv from 8 to 13 March on the question of the just distribution of church buildings. The result was the acceptance of shared practical solutions: the church buildings were divided in the cities of Mykolayiv, Nesteriv, Zolochiv, Yavoriv, Stryi and Boryslav. The protocols for this were signed by the representatives of all four sides. In the declaration of 13 March the members of the commission committed themselves in the name of the churches to rule out any possibility of the violent occupation of the churches; soon afterwards, however, the Greek Catholics left this commission and broke off the process of the peaceful resolution of the conflict which had begun.

The Local Council of the Russian Orthodox Church took place in the Trinity St Sergius Monastery on 7 and 8 June 1990; reference was made in its resolutions to the alarming situation in West Ukraine. It was maintained:

> 19. In evaluating the relations between the Russian Orthodox Church and the Roman Catholic Church the Council had to note with regret that these are seriously burdened by the Uniate problem; and this problem is becoming increasingly acute in West Ukraine.
>
> The legally unregulated situation of the Uniates is a hindrance to the development of brotherly relations between world Orthodoxy and the Roman Catholic Church; it undermines the hope for a successful continuation of the Orthodox-Catholic dialogue.
>
> The Council acknowledges the right of the Union communities to legal existence, but regards the acts of violence against Orthodox clergy and laity and the occupation of Orthodox churches as inadmissible. These actions which are remote from the Christian spirit are being organized and engaged in by individual groups. The Council protests against unconstitutional actions by local authorities of West Ukraine which discriminate against the citizens of the Orthodox confession, involve themselves in the internal matters of the church, and endanger the legal rights of the Orthodox church.
>
> The Council condemns the acts of violence of the Stalin regime against the Greek Catholics and any involvement of the Soviet

authorities in the internal life of the church. The Council regards it as inadmissible to resort to similar methods today with regard to the Orthodox. History has shown that the complicated problem of relations between these two communities is not to be solved by force, by suppression of the legal rights of the Orthodox and Uniates.

20. The Council regrets that the way of normalizing relationships between Orthodox and Catholics of the Eastern rite in Galicia, by regulating the situation of Union communities through the work of the Commission with representatives of the Moscow Patriarchate, the Holy See, the Ukrainian Orthodox Church and the Catholics of the Eastern rite, which has already been begun, has been broken off by the Uniates. The latter bear responsibility for breaking off the conversations and for the failure to implement the solutions which had been worked out by the commission with the agreement of the United church.

After that, aggressive actions by the Uniates intensified, with the occupation of Orthodox church buildings. The Council declares that the course adopted by the representatives of the Union makes the situation more difficult and is leading to the hardening of interconfessional enmity in Galicia. The Council calls upon the Holy See to influence the Ukrainian Catholics of the Eastern rite under its jurisdiction, so that the work of the commission can be resumed.

It is quite clear that this dangerous interconfessional conflict can be settled only by church means, through honest dialogue.

It also has to be noted that after the Greek Catholics left the commission the Greek Catholics made a declaration on 17 March 1990 in which they stated that 'the Ukrainian Catholic Church is the only church in the Ukraine'; thus Metropolitan Volodimir Sterniuk called himself Metropolitan not only of L'viv but also of Kiev and Galicia.

The Moscow Patriarchate again proposed in June to hold an extraordinary meeting to discuss this situation and to find ways towards its normalization. But for reasons beyond the control of the Russian Orthodox Church this meeting did not take place until 10 and 14 September. The delegations of the Holy See, the Moscow Patriarchate, the Ukrainian Orthodox and the Ukrainian Catholic Church gathered in the Danilov Monastery in Moscow, confirmed the 'recommendations' of January and backed the continuation of the work of the commission.

Agreement was reached on the points of the communiqué which had a general character, describing principles of co-operation of the churches for the normalization of Orthodox-Catholic relations in West Ukraine.

The fact that the work of the commission was broken off by the Uniate side in March of this year provoked an extremely negative reaction from the Orthodox and disbelief about the possibility of settling the problem by a dialogue with Catholics of the Eastern rite; and as representatives of all the institutions were present at this extraordinary meeting, the Russian and Ukrainian Orthodox churches proposed to resolve at least two concrete questions. At least one each of the churches occupied by the Catholics of the Eastern rite were to be handed over to the Orthodox bishops of L'viv and Ivano-Frankivsk, so that they had the possibility of celebrating the liturgy and giving pastoral care to the faithful; and the old residence was provisionally to be handed over to the Bishop of L'viv until his new residence was built.

Unfortunately the position of the Uniates and their refusal of any compromise made all the former points of the communiqué agreed upon quite meaningless.

As the Vatican delegation could not oppose the position of the Greek Uniates, the conversations led to a dead end.

There followed on 1 October 1990 the Declaration of the Russian Orthodox Church on the Situation in Relations with the Catholic Church. This stated:[3]

> The Holy Synod of the Moscow Patriarchate notes with bitterness that relations between the Roman Catholic Church and the Moscow Patriarchate, which developed successfully after the Second Vatican Council, have been subjected to severe trial by the attempt to resolve the interconfessional problem in West Ukraine. This situation is taking our relationships to another level and raises the question how one can continue the theological dialogue in this situation. Is it compatible with blatant acts of pressure on the Orthodox, with blasphemies of our holy things on the part of the Ukrainian Catholics of the Eastern rite?

That these words are no exaggeration was confirmed by the occupation of a church in Sambor, in the L'viv area, on 17 October 1990. This event was described in a statement by the Orthodox clergy of this city as follows:

> Since May 1990 the Orthodox had been quietly celebrating in the Church of the Birth of the Mother of God in Sambor. The Ukrainian Catholic Church built a chapel in the local park, talked about building their church and collected money. Through an announcement in the press they collected 150,000 and began to lay the foundation stone. In Sambor there is a former Catholic church building (organ hall). That would have been suitable. Although this building was proposed to them

by the city council, the Catholics turned down the offer. In Sambor there are around 7,000 Catholics as opposed to 21,000 Orthodox (the total population numbers 50,000). Since October there had been calls to occupy the Church of the Birth of the Mother of God in Sambor; in this connection the Catholic priests held street services outside this church and demonstrations which had an anti-Moscow character.

The first church building was occupied by Catholics in the night of 30–31 January 1990. A day later the Orthodox liberated it again. Then the local authorities proposed that the church should be used jointly for worship. The Orthodox asked for guarantees that this church would not fall completely into the hands of the Catholics.

In June 1990, W. Golod, the dean of the church, announced the move of part of the community to the Autocephalous Church. This gave rise to two Orthodox committees which celebrated alternately in the church. Subsequently the authorities asked for the keys of the church and said that they themselves would decide its fate. The Orthodox refused; thereupon the city council prosecuted the Orthodox for breaking the agreement and in order to get hold of the keys. At this time the city council had already made an arrangement with the Catholics for the use of the church.

The Supreme Court of the Ukraine allowed the protest of the state advocate of the Republic, repealed all the judgments of the local authority about the church, and handed it over to the Orthodox. This happened on 21 August 1991.

The day before, 20 August, the local council had registered the Orthodox community as a person in law. On 30 August the same council required the Orthodox to evacuate the church. This decision of the council was not reported to the community.

It should be added that in this summer, on 24 July, about 200 members of the OMON [special security troops] had attacked the church, but the people had protected the church. On 29 August 1991 at 6 a.m. the Catholics broke down the doors of the church and occupied the building. The people liberated the church again. After this seizure, on 30 August the local council resolved that the militia should seal the church and put a guard on it.

On 17 September, around four in the morning, about 47 buses and 3 armoured cars came to the church, which was defended by about 40 people; a further 20 men were with the priests inside the people. 900 OMON people, 24 militia units and a firefighting unit took part in the attack. The leadership consisted of 54 men, headed by Colonel Kret, the deputy chief of the UWD of the L'viv region.

All the defenders of the church were surrounded and driven back to a distance of 200 yards, some cordons were erected, and no one was allowed to approach the church. Tear gas was used. The inner door was torn down and 200 OMON people stormed the church. The guardians were beaten with batons, even in the sanctuary. The wounded were dragged out and thrown into an OMON vehicle. Priest Buchnij had his teeth knocked out and a poor invalid in the first group was terribly mistreated; the same thing happened to war veteran Chaljawko, some young people and around ten women pensioners. An Orthodox woman, Anna Sarachman, was taken to hospital with brain damage and a double fracture of the chin. She was not operated on for three days. All nineteen men who had been in the church were arrested and taken to the militia barracks at Drogobytsch. They included three priests: A.Schewz, I.Schwez and N.Buchnij. They sat there for eleven hours without medical help.

At 2 p.m. the representatives of the Orthodox communities approached the deputy UWD of the L'viv region and asked him what had happened to the prisoners. His answer was: 'Sambor is peaceful and the priests have been taken home.' At this point the Orthodox in Sambor asked for the prisoners to be released; they went to the railway and threw themselves on the tracks; thereupon the prisoners were released at 5 p.m.

Finally, it should be noted that in autumn 1990 the faithful and clergy of the Orthodox church in Ivano-Frankivsk and Ternopil, who had lost all their churches and could not attend any worship, several times resorted to such extreme measures as hunger strikes.

The situation in West Ukraine was discussed by the Moscow Patriarchate in the Joint Commission for Theological Dialogue between the Orthodox local churches and the Roman Catholic Church. At the sixth plenary session in Freising (Germany), which took place between 6 and 16 July, the following statement was agreed upon:[4]

VI.1 As there is tension between the Roman Catholic churches of the Byzantine rite and the Orthodox Church in some regions, the problem of the Union is urgent, and it must have priority over other questions to be considered.

2. In this case the term 'Union' means the effort to attain the unity of the church by splitting the Orthodox communities, regardless of the fact that in ecclesiology the Orthodox Church is a sister church which mediates grace and salvation. In accord with the text of the Vienna sub-

commission, we reject Union as a method of seeking unity, because it does not correspond to the universal tradition of our church.

3. Where it was applied, Union as a method did not serve to bring the churches together. On the contrary, it provoked constantly new divisions. Such a situation was an occasion for unhappiness and struggles which remain in the historical memory of the churches. Moreover ecclesiological motives require a quest for other ways.

4. Now that our churches are meeting on the basis of ecclesiological brotherly communion, union can only destroy the important achievements of dialogue.

VII. However, quite apart from the aim of bringing the historic churches closer together, practical measures are needed to avoid the consequences of the dangerous tension which prevails in many Orthodox regions. The following should be noted:

(a) The religious freedom of persons and communities is not only a right to be respected fully for Christians who enjoy the divine life; it is also the gift of the Spirit for bringing together the body of Christ, for growth in its fullness (Eph.4.16). This freedom ultimately excludes any form of violence, direct or indirect, physical violence or moral pressure. The gifts of the Spirit which always serve the common good (I Cor.12.27), with the brotherly collaboration of pastors, must finally heal the wounds of the past and lead believers to deep and lasting reconciliation which makes possible the prayer which the Lord commanded his disciples...

(c) Any attempt to persuade the faithful of one church to go over to the other – proselytism – must be excluded as a distortion of the work of the pastor. Moreover it is a negative testimony to those who look critically at the new freedom of the churches and are ready to exploit any case of antagonism.

On 12 December 1990 the statement by the Inter-Orthodox Commission for Theological Dialogue between the Orthodox and the Roman Catholic Church was accepted in the Fanar;[5] it was emphasized that 'the present revival of the Union is being accompanied by gross violations of human rights and religious freedom'. The Freising Declaration was also endorsed.

A session of the Co-ordinating Committee of the International Joint Commission for Theological Dialogue between the Orthodox and the Catholic Church was held between 10 and 15 July in Ariccia, Italy. The closing document was accepted, in which it was stated that the rise of the Eastern Catholic churches had 'led to a situation which has become a source of conflict and suffering above all for Orthodox'. The document contained recommendations with an appeal for dialogue as a method of solving problems.

But despite the fact that the dialogue between the Orthodox Churches and the Roman Catholic Church on union as a religious and historical phenomenon was positive, there was virtually no settlement of the conflict. The meeting of the delegations of the Moscow Patriarchate and the Holy See in Geneva on 2 and 3 March 1992 also brought no resolution of events. The communiqué of this meeting states:

> As far as the situation in West Ukraine and in relations between the Orthodox Church and the Ukrainian Greek Catholic Church is concerned, the delegations agreed that the principles formulated jointly in Moscow in 1990 and approved by the Catholic authorities and the hierarchy of the Moscow Patriarchate remain an effective basis for any concern to resolve them, but there continues to be disagreement over the question of what mechanism would be best suited to implement these principles.

Uniatism still remains a problem which hinders dialogue between the Roman Catholic Church and the Russian Orthodox and other Orthodox churches. Metropolitan Kirill of Smolensk and Kaliningrad, President of the Church Foreign Ministry of the Moscow Patriarchate, said in an interview with the journal *La Croix* on 12 March 1991:

> It is not our church but Stalin who banned the Uniates. And without pressure we have received those who remain Orthodox and do not want to become Catholics of the Latin rite or atheists. I was always convinced that when our public life was normalized, the Uniates would certainly have the right to exist. In my view the Greek Catholic Church should give up proselytism and serve as a bridge between West and East.
> But if it is to do that, it should use the theology of the Second Vatican Council in its thought and praxis.

This view can be taken as the general attitude of the hierarchy of the Russian Orthodox Church today.

Notes

1. English text of the communiqué in *The Journal of the Moscow Patriarchate* 1990, 4, 49.
2. English text, ibid., 5, 8f.

3. English text, ibid. 1991, 1, 2-4.
4. English text, ibid. 1990, 10, 46f.
5. Cf. *The Journal of the Moscow Patriarchate* 1991, 4, 57f.

The Second Vatican Council and its Significance for the Russian Orthodox Church

Vitaly Borovoi

1. The Second Vatican Council is a decisive turning point in the history of the Christian world. When Pope John XXIII opened the first session of the Council on 11 October 1962, it was then a council convened for the renewal (*aggiornamento*) of the Catholic Church, but when Pope Paul VI closed the last (fourth) session of this Council on 8 December 1965 it had become a 'Council of Great Hopes' for the whole of the Christian world.

2. Although it was not an ecumenical council in the historical, canonical and dogmatic sense of the term, as had been the seven Ecumenical Councils of the early church (before the division of 1054), many of its results have been received in the contemporary life of many churches, influencing the development of theological thought and contributing towards the radical change and general improvement of climate in relations between churches, confessions and religions throughout the world.

3. These changes, which are beneficial for all, are connected with what is now usually described as 'the revolution of John XXIII' and 'the Eastern policy' (*Ostpolitik*) of Paul VI.

4. The orientation of their pontificates and their personal charisms in the conduct of the Council, like 'the charisms of service' and 'primacy in love' (in the spirit of Ignatius of Antioch), helped the Council fathers to confront basic questions of renewal (*aggiornamento*) in the Catholic Church and bring them to a happy resolution.

5. Both John XXIII and Paul VI were authentically 'angelic popes' *(pastores angelici)*, to use the terminology of medieval prophecy in this context. They dedicated their lives to the great work of the renewal of the Catholic Church, for Christian unity and the affirmation of the peace and brotherhood of peoples all over the world ('that the world may believe'). Hence their so-called 'revolution' and the so-called 'Eastern policy'. John XXIII began this work through an inspiration from on high and Paul VI continued it. This became evident above all in their direction of the Second Vatican Council.

6. In analysing and evaluating the course of the conciliar debates and their influence on the life of the church in the period after the Council, many theologians and historians note that what happened was a real 'Copernican revolution' which put an end to the inertia and immobility of the past and set the life of the churches in motion, so that they began to cope with the problems and demands of modern times. This 'Copernican revolution' is happening all over the world, in the life of all the churches and their peoples, and therefore the conciliar experience of the Catholic Church at Vatican II is of prime importance for all the churches, particularly including our church, which has an acute need for *aggiornamento*.

7. John XXIII and Paul VI saw the Council as the centre and instrument of the renewal (*aggiornamento*) of the inner life of the Catholic Church: of its catechetical methods, missionary activity, liturgical life and internal direction; of the episcopate and the clergy and of monasticism; an *aggiornamento* of social doctrine and the social activity of the church, of relations with the world outside, with non-believers and the Marxist ideology. When he met with the preparatory commission of the Council, John XXIII said (13 September 1960) that its task did not consist in discussing one or other dogmatic principle or canonical rule to find their source in revelation, as the theologians of the past had done; now their task was a different one. There was a need to present the theological truths in the correct interpretation, to restore their original character to them, so that they were capable of filling the life of the peoples with authentic Christian values. According to the pope, the task of the Council would be to expound the truths of dogma and introduce them into the awareness and life of people without modifying them, but in a comprehensible and effective way, so that they would correspond to the needs of the mission of the church in the contemporary world.

8. The pope was particularly preoccupied with the keen desire of conservative political and ecclesiastical circles to use the church and the Council for the political struggle against the Soviet Union and the other Socialist countries. The pope, thinking of the peace and unity of all peoples, decisively rejected such requests and made a direct statement about them in his speech at the opening of the Council: 'But it seems to us that we have to dissent from those prophets of evil and misfortune...Today it is better to seek to recognize the ways of Divine Providence... which with wisdom follows the objective established for the good of the church.'

Contrary to all expectations... 'Divine Providence, and also those manifestations which outwardly seem directed against the aims of the church, can change and be of service to the church.'[1]

9. Inspired by these thoughts and convictions, the pope had published the encyclical *Mater et Magistra* in 1961; this was followed by *Pacem in terris*. The desire to avoid war and to summon everyone to peace and reconciliation had guided the pope at the time of the Berlin crisis in 1961 and the Cuba crisis in 1962. In the meeting of the cardinals of the Curia and the officials of the Vatican Secretariat of State the pope had affirmed that it was necessary to be guided by a neutrality which transcended nationality and to support the UNO, the non-aligned countries and all the forces which would contribute to peace. With regard to the Cuba crisis the pope had told the Secretariat of State that it was necessary to change the orientation of Vatican foreign policy rapidly, to intervene with concrete proposals and peace initiatives, and also to evaluate the question of reconciliation and the normalization of relations with the Socialist countries, in particular with the USSR, Poland, Yugoslavia, Hungary and Czechoslovakia.

10. The leading circles in the Socialist countries, above all in the USSR, much appreciated such peace initiatives by the pope. Khrushchev was one of the first to reply after the pope's appeal on 10 September 1961. He did so through TASS on 28 September, in a very positive way and with a well-argued positive evaluation of the pope's appeal.

In November of the same year Khrushchev sent good wishes to the pope on his eightieth birthday. The pope replied, and even personally revised the text of the reply. Thus began the dialogue between the pope and Khrushchev, a dialogue which continued until 1963. This peace dialogue between the pope and Khruschchev helped our church a good deal in the question of sending our observers to the Council.

11. This is not the place to describe in detail the prelude to our position on the question of sending observers to the Council.

At the time of the pontificate of Pius XII relations with the Vatican and with the Catholic Church were very bad on both the social and political and the ecclesiastical levels. There had been every reason to suppose that if our church received an invitation to the Council, the militant anti-Communism of Pius XII and the unilateral pro-Western orientation of the Vatican would have become a political obstacle to our sending observers.

The motivations of this kind which were at the root of our difficulties are openly formulated in the article *'Non possumus'* (We cannot) in the *Review of the Patriarchate of Moscow*.

12. John XXIII's 'revolution' and his dialogue with Khrushchev helped to overcome these difficulties and opened the way for Rome, for the Council. Next appeared a further obstacle, in addition to the political one, which was ecclesiastical and canonical. It became known that in fact Rome was thinking of the participation by observers from the Orthodox Church in terms of observers sent by Constantinople and through Constantinople, as if Orthodoxy were not made up of autocephalous churches. The reaction of the heads of our church was extremely clear. We are an autocephalous church. If the participation of our observers was desired, we would resolve such a question only after receiving an official invitation addressed by Rome to our church.

13. Monsignor Willebrands came to Moscow bringing complete information about the Council. This visit was followed by an official invitation, and the Synod of our church decided to send observers. As a result of this a clear misunderstanding arose with Constantinople. In taking the decision to send observers, our Synod was certain that Constantinople and the other Orthodox churches would be sending (or more precisely would already have sent) their own observers. When the heads of our church had expressed doubts about the possibility of sending observers, we had felt that we were alone in our refusal. We knew that Constantinople and the other churches supported the opportunity to send observers. And everyone tried to persuade the churches to send them. We replied that we had not received an invitation. We were certain that we had deliberately not been invited for political motives. When finally we were invited, on the very eve of the opening of the Council, we were then in a position to send observers. The Council had already been opened and our observers arrived only after the opening of the Council. Only then did it emerge that Constantinople had been constrained by a series of internal motives to

refuse the invitation to send observers and that it had informed Rome and all the Orthodox churches of this. We received the telegram from Constantinople notifying us of their refusal of the invitation to send observers at a time when, without yet knowing of this decision, our church had already resolved to send observers and had informed all the world of this (Rome, Constantinople, the WCC, the Orthodox churches and others). It was now impossible to go back on our decision. Thus observers from Moscow (whom no one expected) were present at the first session of the Council, but not from Constantinople.

14. In respect of the work of the Council and the presence of observers it should noted that at the Council there was guaranteed:
(a) complete freedom of discussion and examination of all the questions by all those taking part in the Council;
(b) the possibility for all the observers to express their own opinions, make their own observations and state their own feelings at regular meetings with Catholic theologians and those taking part in the Council;
(c) an attitude of extraordinary attention towards the observers by the Secretariat for Unity, the Secretariat of the Council and the communication centre of the Council.

Those in charge of the Council were always ready to defend the observers and the dignity of the Russian Orthodox Church.

15. In this context it should be noted separately that the observers of the Russian Church played an active part in the work of liberating the Uniate Metropolitan Iosif Slipyj. Cardinal Testa had spoken with the observers in the name of the pope about the opportuneness of a freeing of Slipyj. Slipyj was now very old and moreover was sick. It would be a humane gesture to release him from prison and give him the possibility of ending his days quietly in Rome. In Rome Slipyj would not engage in any official activity and would not make any political statements. The pope would be 'very, very, and quite concretely grateful' for such a humanitarian act on the part of the Soviet government.

Testa had asked the observers to report this conversation to Moscow, to the patriarchate. The observers wrote a report. When he was freed and settled in the Vatican, Slipyj recalled that after he had been liberated and had received permission to go to Rome and live there under the protection of the pope, the Russian church had participated in the organization of his departure from Moscow together with Monsignor Willebrands.

This active collaboration in the liberation of Slipyj had demonstrated to Rome that the heads of the Orthodox Church had trusted the assurances of the pope and that they sincerely wanted to remove obstacles in the way of an improvement of reciprocal relations, using the Council and the Slipyj affair as possibilities for a certain rapprochement with Rome. Contacts of Soviet government circles with the Vatican also encouraged it.

The high esteem in which John XXIII had come to be held in the eyes of Moscow with his politics of peace and reconciliation had shown the Russian church the green light in closer church relations with Rome.

16. John XXIII's successor Paul VI continued his great work in a worthy and faithful way. John XXIII had reawakened a stagnant church and had brought it to the Council, whereas Paul VI, at the cost of enormous efforts, having overcome all the antagonisms which existed within the Council and around it, and having maintained unity, succeeded in bringing the Council to a happy conclusion. Here Paul VI was really a great poet. It was said of him that he possessed Pius XII's shrewdness and John XXIII's charism of wisdom and goodness.

These expectations were fully realized both in the way in which Paul VI guided the Council and in his relations with us, with our church and our country, in what has been called his 'Eastern policy'. This last was a continuation, a development and a deepening of the line taken by John XXIII.

17. I shall not say much here about Paul VI's 'eastern policy', since it is well known. Much has been said and written on it. Among some it found assent and recognition, and among others criticism and condemnation.

Many people in the West thought that the views of Paul VI and his Secretary of State Cardinal Casaroli on the normalization of relations between the Vatican and the Socialist countries (Yugoslavia, Hungary and above all the USSR) were 'a capitulation to the East' in the face of the 'Communist threat'.

18. However, a careful analysis of the 'revolution' of John XXIII and the 'Eastern policy' of Paul VI furnishes every reason for arriving at a diametrically opposed conclusion. This was not a 'capitulation' to Communism and the USSR nor a 'sell out', nor ideological disarmament in the face of the Soviet system of the so-called 'Socialist camp' in Eastern and Central Europe. On the contrary, it was a reasonable and deliberate substitution of unjustified bellicose and primitive forms of anti-Communism and political anti-Sovietism from the 1940s and 1950s by changing them into more flexible and more effective ideological and diplomatic efforts to weaken the external and internal dynamic of the Soviet system

(from within the Socialist camp) by means of domestication and assimilation. Attempts were made by means of dialogue in spheres of common interest to tone down the bitterness of the opposition through talking; attempts were made to Christianize the atheistic Soviet system by means of a civil and amicable diplomacy. This policy was not established suddenly, but in the course of historical transformations. And now we can witness the fruits of the line taken by John XXIII and Paul VI, as witnesses to and participants in the dismantling of the Soviet totalitarian system and the birth of a new free Europe through Christian testimony, a European community extending from the Atlantic to the Urals (with an extension in the narrow space of Eurasia as far as China, Japan and Alaska).

These are the historical fruits of John XXIII's 'revolution' and Paul VI's 'Eastern policy'.

19. Alongside this we must always remember that Paul VI had to continue John XXIII's 'revolution' and realize his own 'Eastern policy' in situations which were far more difficult than those of his great predecessor. The new pope did not yet enjoy the enormous popularity and authority which John XXIII had gained. In the conservative circles of the church there was now widespread mistrust and fear of the consequences of the *aggiornamento*.

20. At the beginning of his pontificate Paul VI had to guide the Council and bring the work of its complex mechanism to a conclusion. This was far more complex and difficult than it had been for Pope John XXIII at the time of the first session of the Council, when the opposition to the Council was not yet organized. However, when at the end of the first session the general orientation of John XXIII's 'revolution' had become more or less clear, different and opposed theological points of view emerged and began to spread in the Catholic Church in connection with the role of the church in society and the state. This led to pluralism, contrasts and confrontations both in the work of the conciliar commissions and in the Council itself. The pope had to be a wise helmsman capable of steering the ship of the church between the Scylla of conservative integralism and the Charybdis of revolutionary reforms, in the direction of the *aggiornamento* indicated by John XXIII. Shrewd discernment in evaluations, prudent reflection in decisions and reasonable patience in procedures helped Paul VI to lead the church out of the crisis and to confront and overcome the subsequent period of challenge.

This had a great and indeed decisive significance for creating trust and bringing an improvement in our attitude towards Rome (and in our relations with it).

21. The heads of the Russian Orthodox Church trusted the good will of Pope John XXIII and the sincerity and effectiveness of the 'Eastern policy' of Paul VI. They trusted the positive changes within the Catholic Church and enthusiastically welcomed the fraternal spirit and atmosphere of renewal towards Orthodoxy indicated in the ecumenical decisions, of the Second Vatican Council. Such a completely positive valuation had valid foundations and was based on the fundamental principles and interests of our church.

22. It is not possible in a brief article to go in detail into our positions in evaluating the theological content of the discussions at the Council and the Council documents, and making an analysis of individual formulations, particularly those of the Constitution *Gaudium et Spes* (on The Church in the Modern World), the decree on the missionary activity of the church and the decrees on the apostolate of the laity and on freedom of conscience.

23. I shall say simply that we welcomed with pleasure the ecumenical and social role of the Council documents and pinned our greatest hopes on them.

No one had such need of freedom of conscience and the possibility for social activity and missionary educational activity on the part of the church as we did. And no one in the world suffered so much for lack of all this as we did.

This was about the concrete problems of our everyday life. We were profoundly interested in their advancement in the life of the international community. Our approaches to the World Council of Churches and the Catholic Church, our entry into all the aspects of the world ecumenical movement, were bound up with our hopes of survival and of a change in our situation. However, we had to be prudent and shrewd, reflecting on every decision and every step, just as Paul VI did.

For us these were the hard times of Khrushchev's attack on the church.

It was for this reason, too, that we joined the World Council of Churches in Geneva and sent observers to the Second Vatican Council in Rome. We needed to exploit all this to the maximum in favour of the church, but in such a way as not to make false moves and mistakes which would lose openings and ways for the church through which links and also communion with universal Christianity would develop, bringing back for the church times of isolation from the rest of the world like those under Stalin.

24. The Catholic Church and the Second Vatican Council had an enormous social and political significance on an international scale. The influence of the events of the Council and the role which they played in the subsequent development of the Catholic Church and in determining its positions on many difficult problems posed by the modern world were a question of prime importance for us.

This could help, but it could also cause considerable damage, almost do more damage than bring help. Taking account of this, with all our hearts we welcomed the shrewd prudence and balanced aims which marked the line taken by Paul VI both within the Council and outside it. We were not in fact concerned that the work of the council should proceed hastily and arrive at a rapid conclusion. Too hasty a resolution could lead (and did lead) to tense situations in the Council and in the Catholic Church outside it. Tense situations only lead to struggles between opposed forces, make them worse and drive them towards extremism. Were this to have happened, we could have been involved in such struggle against our will, not only as a passive victim but with the risk of becoming a pawn in a game which was not ours and hostages of our own reality. Our bitter historical experience bears witness to this possibility. Such an experience demonstrated that our prime need was to be concerned for our church and our faithful, who were confessing Christ in difficult and oppressive conditions in our society at that time.

25. The balanced and thoughtful way in which the meetings of the Council and the external activity of the Catholic Church were being conducted at that time instilled in us a certainty that we would not suffer harm; on the contrary, they helped to overcome our problems, both at home and abroad. This produced an extremely positive attitude and assessment among our church leaders and 'in Soviet social and political circles' also led to a calm (even encouraging) attitude towards our rapprochement with Rome.

26. For this reason, too, all welcomed with satisfaction the fact that the Second Vatican Council ended with a radical change on the question of rapprochement and reconciliation between Orthodox and Catholics. The anathemas of 1054 were annulled and a beginning was made on a 'dialogue of love'. Fraternal meetings and visits of popes and patriarchs, metropolitans, cardinals, bishops, theologians and so on developed from both sides. Here was the start of a cordial rapprochement between Constantinople and Rome, but also a cordial rapprochement, co-operation and bilateral dialogue between Moscow and Rome.

27. Great hopes had arisen among the Orthodox for the joint Orthodox-Catholic Commission for Theological Dialogue, which aimed at re-establishing eucharistic communion and consequently full *koinonia* between the sister Catholic and Orthodox Churches.

28. There were also widespread hopes among the Orthodox of the further development in the Catholic Church of a system of collegial and conciliar government of the church on the part of the college of bishops – the successors of the apostles. It looked as if the Bishop of Rome might become the one who has the primacy and who presides in love (in the spirit of Ignatius of Antioch) within the college (council) of his brother Catholic bishops; these in their turn also being, like the pope, successors of the apostles, would exercise *episcope* (the episcopal ministry) in their local churches and eparchies in the spirit of conciliarity (*sobornost'*) and unity. This fully corresponds to the Orthodox conception of conciliarity (*sobornost'*) in the One Holy Conciliar and Apostolic Church.

29. Hopes were also nurtured by the Orthodox Church of a further development in the Catholic Church of conferences of bishops, which would lead to the re-establishment or formation of local Catholic churches in the various countries and regions of the Catholic world. The hope was that these local churches would become autonomous churches in conciliar unity with one another and together in unity, with the Bishop of Rome as their primate, with their pope-patriarch of the West and head of the Catholic Church.

30. The Russian Orthodox Church had taken part in this process of reconciliation and rapprochement with the Catholic Church on an equal footing with Constantinople and with all the other Orthodox Churches.

Such good and close relations had been established between Moscow and Rome that this fact had even aroused discontent and misunderstanding within the church and outside it.

31. So it is that after thirty years of rapprochement and cordial dialogue, the 'sister churches' have entered into a period of crisis in their relations.

32. This change, which is sad for both parties, is a consequence of the crisis of the spirit of Vatican II within the Catholic Church in respect of the Orthodox and of a return to outdated methods of promoting union and proselytism in the Orthodox countries of Eastern Europe and the Middle East. That could not fail to provoke a crisis of trust in the Catholic Church

among the Orthodox. This has also given rise to the Orthodox reaction of self-defence, particularly in the Russian Orthodox Church, in the light of the complete destruction of Orthodoxy in Galicia (West Ukraine), the artificial introduction of a 'Neo-Union' in Byelorussia, and the deliberately organized activity of missionary proselytism among the Orthodox of the Russian Orthodox Church.

33. Given this present crisis in relations between the Orthodox Church and the Catholic Church in Ukraine, in Byelorussia and in the Russian Federation, alarming questions are being asked about the prospects for a renewal of dialogue and co-operation.

The Orthodox Church firmly believes in the possibility and necessity of re-establishing good friendly fraternal and ecumenical relations and in the continuation of a serious dialogue on an equal footing with the aim of arriving at 'eucharistic communion' between the sister churches.

However, the return to outdated methods of promoting union and of proselytism are an insurmountable obstacle on this way.

Our church formulated its position in the following way in its declaration of 8 October 1991:

> With the advent of freedom for the church, the spirit of brotherhood and ecumenical co-operation has begun to disappear from inter-confessional relations. This is being replaced, disgracefully, by an almost manifest proselytism which is resulting in almost open aggression that threatens to turn into a religious war. This is not just a strongly emotive statement. Events are taking place quite blatantly in Ukraine, in the Western regions, whose Orthodoxy has almost been destroyed, in which violence and extortion are the basic arguments of the Greek Catholic side. Having caused the failure of the quadripartite negotiations at the beginning of 1990, the Uniate party has rejected the principle of dialogue and set out on the disastrous road of the continuation of the conflict which has virtually compromised even the very idea of dialogue.

34. However, the Orthodox side has not abandoned dialogue, but is ready to continue it with the aim of normalizing and improving relations. The declaration states:

> We are not closing the door to fraternal dialogue, and bear witness to our faithfulness to this way as the only method of resolving the problems between our churches. But this dialogue must consider these questions, which are very painful and burning ones. Resolving them can really serve to improve relations between our churches.

This has also been confirmed by the declaration of the Inter-Orthodox Commission which has expressed the view of the Fullness of Orthodoxy (at the Fanar, on 12 December 1990):

> The dialogue which is taking place between the Orthodox Churches and the Catholic Church must become an effective mechanism for overcoming the problems which are arising among the churches because of the revival of Uniatism. This question is dangerously perverting the very aims of the dialogue. It is utterly clear that without a positive solution to this question all the efforts of the Orthodox and the Catholic directed towards the development of relations between them and the achievement of the aims of the dialogue will prove vain.

35. Adopting this bitter 'declaration' in the year of the thirtieth anniversary of Vatican II, all the participants in the Inter-Orthodox Commission without doubt recalled the years of the Council 'of the Great Hopes', when it seemed that the time of a great reconciliation would arrive, while the shadows of hatred and isolation from the past would retreat.

However, the past does not easily disappear, and now with great displeasure we are again beginning to talk about and to dispute over Union, the Unitates and Uniatism, while the return in reciprocal relations to old methods and to continual recriminations about the past and continuous recollections of this past are extremely damaging to both parties. They are nothing but narcotics or, even worse, a ghastly food which continuously poisons the self-consciousness and the life of both churches.

36. Today, if we are to put an end to all this, we must return to the times of the Second Vatican Council and resume the process of reconciliation which began in those years. This process was interrupted under the influence of the temptation to exploit Gorbachev's perestroika and the dissolution of the Soviet Union with a view to a rapid and violent re-establishment of Uniatism in the territories in which it had previously been disseminated and with a view to an organized proselytism in the new post-Soviet regions.

An authentic reconciliation, which is more secure and stable, cannot be sustained in the long term if one of the parties in a historical situation which is favourable to it exploits the tragic and unfortunate condition of the other party in order to impose an artificial and unilateral reconciliation on it.

The history of the church offers examples of such imposed reconciliation, which are artificial and of short duration. However, it also knows and can point to examples and models of authentic, sincere and voluntary reconciliation.

In our joint efforts to achieve reconciliation between Orthodox and Catholics we must avoid methods of imposition, but must rather look to examples of authentic and sincere reconciliation and unity.

The Unions (of Florence and Brest) can serve as examples of imposed unity.

However, the experience and the historical examples of the early church can serve as models of authentic reconciliation and unity.

37. The Second Vatican Council must be for all of us an orientation and an inspiration in the perspective of an authentic reconciliation and unity. This Council made the Catholic Church change direction, and with it the whole of the Christian world, directing it towards a theological renewal within, towards pan-Christian ecumenical efforts bound up with this renewal, and towards a quest common to all ways and all models of reconciliation and unity.

Notes

1. The quotations in inverted commas are the author's free adaptation of John XXIII, *Gaudet Mater Ecclesia* 8 and 9.

Towards a Common Future?

Giuseppe Alberigo

Before the end of the 1980s very few people in the West were aware of the survival of a Christian church in the USSR. It is not difficult to recall how surprised people were when in October 1962 two Russian prelates designated by the Patriarchate of Moscow arrived in Rome to take part in the Second Vatican Council as observers. The great majority suspected rather that this was a political manoeuvre on the part of the Khrushchev regime; it seemed improbable that after almost half a century of Soviet rule, which proclaimed its atheist inspiration and made the struggle against religion and the church a key point in its own policy, the Russian church had not just been reduced to a shadow, a tool of the government's plans for hegemony.

Only slowly, and even today perhaps by no means clearly, has awareness developed of two major misunderstandings. The first was the biassed way in which the main Western information centres accepted the anti-religious Soviet propaganda. What better argument against Communism was there than a denunciation of the fight of the Moscow regime against the church? It was too good an opportunity to miss, even at the cost of prematurely attributing to the Soviet atheism, which was undeniable, the success of having killed off the church and the Christian faith in Russia. But was this really the case?

The second misunderstanding consisted in the inveterate Catholic (and perhaps also Western) vice of arguing that the Russian church was essentially subordinate to the political power to the degree that it was unable to survive the end of Tsarist power and its replacement with a hostile political power. Already in the first years after the 1917 October Revolution, Rome had cultivated the hope of a collapse of the Moscow Patriarchate, to the point of making contact with representatives of the Soviet power with a view to a 'Catholicization' of Russia. When the Soviet regime then became consolidated and showed an orientation which was hostile not only to the Orthodox Church but also to any form of Christianity whatsoever, Rome played a key function in the struggle against this regime and – as a function of this struggle – exploited the end of Christianity in the Soviet empire.

In this way the stereotype of an 'atheistic' or at least 'a-Christian' Russia became crystallized in Western culture. This stereotype found a decisive foundation in the predominantly (if not totally) institutional conception of the church which had become established above all in the Catholic world. The conviction had grown that a church which could not enjoy support, or at least benevolent neutrality, from the political power; which could not have visible (and authoritative) public structures – churches, property, schools, seminaries; and which could not express itself in solemn acts, had not only suffered as a church but had also lost its faith. Even where there were no explicit statements to this effect, in general the conviction was that church was the equivalent of the faith.

Above all with perestroika and the fall of the Berlin Wall, the West discovered that Christianity had not disappeared in Russia; that tens of millions of people of every generation and every class were Christian; that the transmission of the faith had not been interrupted; that belief and prayer had never ceased. It was true that the church had suffered every kind of oppression and persecution; that the political power had been programmatically hostile to it; that it had been denied public structures like churches, property, schools and seminaries; that it had not been able to express itself in solemn acts; that the Christians as such had been persecuted in underhand and oppressive ways. But the Christian faith had still been handed down with integrity, though deprived of every aid and even reduced to essentials by the hostility of the public powers. It was a 'naked' faith.

Paradoxically, Western public opinion – which is ideologically, if not theologically, Christian – had unconsciously shared the materialist conviction that the faith could not survive without being supported by institutional structures.

But the new visibility of the Holy Russian Church cannot be just a matter of information. Even more than in the past the Russian 'Orthodox' tradition is a crucial dimension of Christianity and the universal church; it is one of its elements without which the other traditions – Roman, Byzantine, Reformed, Anglican – would be the poorer. Yet communion between these traditions is not without its problems.

First with the pontificate of John XXIII and then with the Second Vatican Council there was an epoch-making shift in Roman Catholicism and, indirectly, in Western Christianity. This change also led to a new look at the other Christian churches, especially the Russian church, which for decades had been caught up in the radical opposition of the Roman pontificate to the Soviet regime. It is important to remember that at that time there were important external reasons for the disintegration of the Soviet empire and the manifestation of perestroika in the 1980s. The continued *Ostpolitik* of Paul VI stabilized and encouraged these developments. The election of a Slavonic prelate as Bishop of Rome around twenty years ago was a starting point for this attention, and began an important elevation of traditions which had long been marginalized.

As we approach the end of the millennium, relations between the Western churches and the Russian church present prospects and problems which deserve maximum attention.

It is all too easy to assert that the Russian tradition is complementary to the Western traditions (other than the Byzantine tradition), but it is very difficult to deepen this complementarity. This is because the marked originality of the Russian interpretation of the Christian faith has generated a tradition with a marked identity and a tendency to see its gospel as the only authentic one. Its periodical anti-ecumenical phases are clearly a heightened form of this awareness, above all when they are associated with nationalistic claims. On the other side the Christians of the West fluctuate between the temptation to 're-evangelize' Russia and the risk of resolving relations in a 'pietistic' admiration for icons and Russian mysticism. Taking account of the Russian tradition and its great spiritual and theological tendencies is a task which has hardly begun to be tackled.

For its part, the Patriarchate of Moscow is committed to cope with fascinating and demanding problems. First of all a reconstruction of the church is in process after the upheavals of Soviet oppression and the war,[1] in all its dimensions and articulations, from church personnel to the material structures and to missionary activity. However, this reconstruction does not want to be dominated by the past, but inspired by tradition and directed toward the future. At the episcopal council at the end of 1994 these problems were confronted organically.[2] Given their particular interest, in an appendix I have included long extracts from the final report of Patriarch Alexis II.[3] The interesting decision to promote the development of a social concept in the Russian Orthodox Church also deserves to be emphasized.

What seem to come together in this unexpected orientation are the post-ideological disorientation prevalent in Russian society and perhaps also the criticisms which have been directed towards the 'angelism' of Orthodoxy along with the example of the Catholic Church, in which Pope Wojtyla has relaunched the importance of the 'social doctrine'. The episcopal council –

with its view that the doctrine of the church is 'above the contingent' – thought it necessary to preface this development with some general doctrinal propositions: the church as a divine-human organism; the nature of this world; the presence and action of the church in the world; the consecration and transformation of the world by the church. It then attached prime importance to the theme of relations between the church and the state, which are such a burning issue in Russian tradition. The church reaffirmed its readiness to co-operate with the state power in the framework of any system of state action, respecting the principle of state secularization and religious freedom, along with the freedom of choice of the individual and the freedom of the state to stimulate a choice which is useful to the individual and to society, and to defend the freedom of the individual from outside pressure. It was also necessary to focus on the problems of the family (divorce, one-parent families, links between the generations in the family, the position of the man and the woman, women's work, and so on); of bioethics (genetic engineering, abortion, contraception, euthanasia, the death penalty, etc.); the spread of eroticism and pornography; lines of demarcation in morality and the action of secular law in such questions); and ecology. Other problematical sectors were those relating to work, property, and war and peace.

Ecumenism in difficulties

The lapse of time since the impulses provided by Pope John and the *aggiornamento* promoted by the Second Vatican Council on the one hand, and the collapse of the ideological struggle after the end of Soviet power on the other, have weakened the ecumenical longing which characterized the 1960s and 1970s. In the long term the myriad of bilateral or multilateral theological discussions has given an impression of inconclusiveness, if not sterility. Integralist or fundamentalist movements are emerging; the practice of proselytism seems to be recurring; and the method of brotherly relations – which has never formally been disowned – is giving place with alarming frequency to competitive and even bullying methods.

This is the basis for the resurgence of tensions almost everywhere between the Orthodox Churches and the Catholic Uniate churches, with a consequent crisis for working parties between these churches, and also for the most recent painful conflict between Moscow and Constantinople over Estonia. These are alarming symptoms of a general slackening in spiritual watchfulness, which highlight the risk of a return to the climate of the 1950s!

It seems increasingly urgent to regain a more serene and constructive inner attitude, allying this with appropriate methods of research and evaluation. It is in fact an illusion to think that it will be possible to emerge from the climate of conflict and competition with the voluntarism of a preference for what unites or what divides. The weight and the viscosity of centuries of rancorous opposition and controversial polemic are dragging down the spirit and the thought of Christians and their churches.

Contrary to all appearances, the quest for what is held in common is not easy to pursue. This is not only because today it implies an abandonment of the quarrels and the animosity which inspires and inflates them, making them seem like the necessary safeguarding of respective identities. The discovery of what unites in fact calls for a rigorous discipline and a sincere effort at research to bring out not only equivalent elements but also above all to rediscover the reciprocal complementarity of diversity which exists yet is not contradictory. That calls for the courage and also the patience to 'open up the spaces of love', to quote a fascinating phrase of Augustine's.[4]

Vatican II was of great importance in changing the climate of inter-Christian relations, more as an event of communion than through the constitutions and degrees that the Council approved. Yet too often the reception has stopped at the corpus of its decisions, with the effect of leaving in the shade the global importance of the Council as a great symphony of diversity, resulting from the commitment of all in communion, assisted by the Spirit. Perhaps it was inevitable that the quest for unity would proceed patchily, and in fits and starts. This is in fact what has happened: from the meeting between Paul VI and Athenagoras to the annulling of the excommunications of 1054, from the various 'mixed working parties' to the ever more numerous theological dialogues and the annual week of prayer, and the innumerable initiatives in encounter and common commitment at the grass roots. In the 1970s this had predominantly positive effects, bearing witness to the fruitfulness of the new ecumenical season, under the discreet direction of centres like the Roman Secretariat, Faith and Order in Geneva and the Department for Foreign Affairs in Moscow.

When by the middle of the 1980s the initial impulse had faded out almost completely, activity remained limited to theological discussions and the centripetal motion towards unity was slowing down to a standstill, with the ultimate risk of entering a phase of 'lukewarmness' (in the sense of the saying in the book of Revelation). The spasms of misunderstanding, of proselytism, of an inability of each side to read the other's hearts which we have been watching for a decade now are causing disorientation. What is disconcerting is not that problems are appearing; that is normal. It is that the problems are being experienced and confronted predominantly in a confessional spirit, with jealous claims of what is 'one's own' (or is held to be such). Each side takes refuge in traditional securities, rejecting the effort to work together to face up to the gospel.

Now that the false euphoria is over, it can be understood better that the quest for what unites is not without its price. It calls for a true *metanoia*, i.e. penitence and conversion. Hitherto the churches had seemed sensitive to the demand to recognize their past faults, but now they are deaf to the demands of changes which will ensure that they avoid committing new faults.

Does not attention to the signs of the times prompt a rediscovery of the incarnation as the acceptance of diversity, as change with diversity? Are we not called on to actualize the dynamic of the procession in the Trinity as a superior analogy to a free and respectful relationship between those who are different, a relationship in which unity and diversity are not subordinate, far less alternative and conflictual?

The time is ripe for a reappropriation of the mystery of the Trinity as a inexhaustible fount of riches, a model for the earthly Jerusalem as much as for the heavenly. We need to attain the complexity of the Trinity, beyond metaphysical and essentialist presuppositions which might prevent us from grasping its dynamic import. All the ecumenical authorities are based on Jesus' invocation 'Holy Father, keep those whom you have given me in your name, that they may be one even as we are one' (John 17.11); yet usually this is understood only as a call to unity, obscuring the pluralistic dimension which is just as central, and even more explicit, in vv.21–22.

The heightening of certainty and stability in the structures of the church and its concrete life is difficult to reconcile with a recognition of the unpredictable breath of the Spirit and the correlative dynamic of the charisms. The church *mater et magistra* risks taking the place of the one Lord and the Spirit. The very way of understanding the faith proves to be profoundly influenced by this eclipse of pneumatology, since it puts in first place the adherence of the faithful to the church and to the formulations of its magisterium, rather than the accord of individuals and communities with the divine gift.

Unity without *metanoia*?

It now seems necessary to ask ourselves about the plausibility of an ecumenical strategy which points in first place to the overcoming of the doctrinal differences, and to challenge the conviction that the causes of the divisions are theological. The proposition that 'theological *dissent* divided the churches and only theological *consent* can unite them' seems less and less convincing. It is in fact based on a heightened perception of one of the causes of the divisions between Christians, which is in turn based on a fossilized conception of Christianity and the churches that emphasizes the doctrinal factors to the point of making them – at least implicitly – coextensive with faith and the church.

The priority given to theological dissent (from the *filioque* to unleavened bread, from justification to *sola Scriptura*, the sacraments and even the prerogatives of the Bishop of Rome) depends on keeping doctrinal formulations central, to the point of making them the very essence of the church. But does this have an adequate basis in the New Testament? Is it not rather the historical product of the encounter of Christianity with a particular culture and its dissociation from it, based on the superiority of the abstract to the concrete, of the concept to reality, of the universal to the particular? On the other hand, the conception of Christianity as truth, rather than as adherence to and discipleship of the person of God's Christ, has for centuries been allied with an organic ecclesiology.

The commitment to renew the unity of the churches by means of doctrinal agreements presupposes a vision of Christianity and the church which puts at the centre doctrinal truth, i.e. a conceptual whole (improperly termed the *depositum fidei*), developed above all by the ancient church in accordance with cultural canons which it received from classical civilization. These canons were made increasingly rigid and intransigent by the way in which Christians differed from pagan society, and in confrontations with the adherents of the classical religions. The doctrinal nature of the great conflicts experienced by the early church led to the faith being expressed and made recognizable and communicable above all by means of theological elaborations. This came to be affirmed as a common denominator of the church communities, constituted by doctrinal formulations. We know that reference to these formulations progressively marginalized the importance of holiness as factors in communion. There was an increasing preference for univocal theological elaborations, favoured by the cultural homogeneity of Mediterranean Christianity.

The multicultural aspect of contemporary Christianity and the urge of ordinary Christians to overcome the state of passivity in the life of the church have shattered that conception, obviously not in the sense of denying any importance to theological doctrine and its formulations, but by affirming a richer, articulated and dynamic vision of Christianity and the church. The global discipleship of Christ and his gospel has regained ecclesial (and no longer just personal and private) importance, in its two aspects of the life of the Christian communities and the brotherly sharing of the human condition in the company of other men and women. This has led to a reshaping of the importance of the doctrinal dimension – and even more of dogmatic formulations – over against the other dimensions of Christian faith and life. Parallel to this, the function of the clergy has also been relativized, making it essentially a service within the ecclesial community (and not *above* it).

It is interesting to emphasize two consequences of this development here. In the first place the monolithic and one-dimensional acceptance of Christian truth has been overcome; it is recognized that the criterion of authenticity is the person of Jesus the Christ, in all the depth of his mystery, and not a particular internal conceptual coherence. According to this point of view, knowledge of the truth is mobile, and therefore historical, not ahistorical, up to the parousia; it comes about through partial approximations which are complementary rather than exclusive and alternative. Secondly, there are glimpses that the great church is not co-extensive with doctrine, which does not constitute even its most important dimension, if it is true that the church is a communion of living stones, a body in continuous development towards a final transfiguration. Adherence to doctrine, and above all to a particular doctrinal formulation, can no longer be the ultimate criterion for determining membership of the *Una sancta*.

In the light of this, is it not inadequate – at the same time both too much and too little – to focus unity essentially on the doctrinal dimension, which is almost inevitably understood in a monolithic and monocultural way, as a jealously-guarded possession? Does it not involve the whole being of the church, from Abel to the last of the righteous? Is it not necessary to bring together in the way of union all the ecclesial dimensions, all the charisms which each church has received, including the sinners which have weighed it down and disfigured it?

Does not a remembrance that unity and reform of the church cannot be dissociated, though that was vainly attempted on the eve of the Council of Florence and then on the eve of the Council of Trent, mean that the quest for the *Una sancta* cannot consist only in the theological mending of old rents, but implies a readiness of the churches for *metanoia*? This must be a *metanoia* which by its very nature involves all the dimensions of the church in a critical confrontation with the gospel and the signs of the times, the symptoms and markers of the emergence of the 'today' of the gospel and its directions. Again, does not the doctrinal understanding of the unity of the church today imply an inappropriate interpretation of the Niceno-Constantinopolitan marks of the church for which unity, instead of being linked to holiness, catholicity and apostolicity – though facets of the heavenly Jerusalem – is disconnected from them and assumed to be independent. Are not the notes, rather, interdependent within an 'economic' vision?

The separation, which has almost always been crystallized over a long period, has marked each church, leading it to emphasize its own identity in order to make up for and cover the impoverishment to which the division has led. So it is necessary for the quest for unity to involve and bring into play the whole church, and not only the points where there has manifestly been a rift.

It is equally important to recognize that the united church cannot be simplistically imagined as the sum of the divided churches with the causes of conflict removed: in other words, the repristination of the situation before the break in communion. If this were the case, the loss of unity would only be an institutional occurrence, and not an event which mysteriously has its roots in the history of salvation. To engage in the movement towards the union of the churches therefore means being open to a new and unknown outcome, determined by the Spirit far more than by the will of the churches. This calls for making the most of the whole spiritual heritage accumulated by faith, patiently recognizing the (partial) authenticity of the individual traditions, and therefore their legitimacy and their compatibility in the economy of the proclamation of salvation. Why engage in confrontation on the points of difference and not rather begin, in the power of the communion of saints, to share the manifold gifts and talents that we have received? Finally, last but not least, the way of unity also calls for discernment about the ultimate nature of Christian unity, which is not an institutional 'mark', nor even just a historical characteristic, but is essentially an eschatological dimension, as is indicated by the whole of John 10, where the one flock and the one shepherd is clearly a characteristic of the kingdom.

To recognize the eschatological nature of the unity of Christians does not in fact imply a fatalistic acceptance of the divisions, but calls for a keen sense of the limits. Unity cannot be pursued in accordance with the model of secular societies and above all modern states, as a visible unity of aims and means on the basis of a common geographical, historical and linguistic denominator. The one church can only be the shared dwelling of believers, fit to safeguard their communion, fed by the Spirit in love and in the power of the cross.

The way to Jerusalem can only be gradual and slow, joyful and tiring at the same time; visible and concrete, but also mysterious and inward, and therefore an endless process in the course of which even the most significant events are stages and not finishing posts. Frequently, however, even within the ecumenical movement, a simplified understanding of unity has developed – completely 'historical' – as a result to be attained once and for all. According to this schematic point of view, the impressive degrees of unity which already exist are neglected, as though they were irrelevant to the quest for unity. This has the effect of excessively magnifying the elements of diversity, which are quickly seen as causes of division. Perhaps it is necessary to look again at the whole eschatological depth of the unity of the church, avoiding the risk of an ecumenical triumphalism which fluctuates between steps so small as to seem immobility, and excessive and definitive aims which are to be achieved in utopia.

It can be fruitful to recognize that the churches are labouring to develop an ecclesial understanding of *metanoia* which is both timely and evocative. It seems that the criteria and methods of conversion have been irremediably confined to the sphere of individual ascesis. To loosen the bond which has been created between the unity of each church and its concrete mode of existence appears hard. Even the age-old *reformatio ecclesia* needs to be thought of in an eschatological perspective rather than as a call for renewal on the basis of an ideal ecclesial model.

Towards a 'pastoral ecumenism'

Does not perhaps the experience triggered off by Vatican II call for a 'pastoral ecumenism', capable of transcending the impasse in which the quest for doctrinal agreement is stuck? But what does 'pastoral ecumenism' mean? If this is not to be just verbal sleight of hand but an evocative formula, there is need for a commitment to free and bold research which identifies its aim, content and method. I am convinced that pastoral ecumenism is a fruitful perspective in which to put both the faith experienced by the ecclesial communities and their capacity to bear witness – in a transparent way – to Christ for the sisters and brothers of the diverse societies and cultures of today. It is an attitude not 'for oneself' but 'for the others', which is already present in so many members of the different 'divided' Christian churches. These vestiges of the authentic great church must be recognized in the unity which brings them together and must form the nucleus and the ferment of the *Una Sancta* and a renewed ecumenical theology.

To leave doctrinal ecumenism behind will mean departing from the context in which it was born, though it performed a decisive function in the overcoming of the controversialist stage. At that time it was vital for the very survival of the ecumenical perspective to overcome the heat of controversy by means of a reflective attitude, but that is now increasingly showing its limits. On the other hand, perhaps this risk was not a dominant factor in the parallel institutionalization of Life and Work and Faith and Order.

The crucial nub of this 'pastoral ecumenism' is constituted by the reality and the theology of *koinonia* around which the pledge to engage in a courageous radical renewal must be expressed.

If the Christian experiences of the past undeniably condition the future with the weight of their achievements and their mistakes, they also bring liberation. In fact they bear witness to the partiality and therefore the inadequacy of every experience relating to the totality of the mystery of revelation and the many-sided riches of the church. Seen in the span of two millennia, the Christian experience of *koinonia* shows an alternation of systole and diastole, i.e. of contractions and dilations. This awareness allows us to recover intact the trust in the generative force of Christian testimony within any human condition.

Appendix

The Mission of the Russian Church Today

Patriarch Aleksi II[5]

One problem today is disturbing many priests and lay people in our church. This is how to make accessible to our contemporaries, with a view to mission, the liturgical life and every form of Orthodox ecclesial culture generally.

As is well known, for long decades the transmission of ecclesial culture was maintained solely within the framework of a few rare communities, transformed by the atheistic power into kinds of ghettos. The majority of our compatriots have lost a feeling for the transmission and development of Orthodox culture.

The cultural means used by the church in the past are seen by the new converts as vestiges of an ethnographic kind or, at the other extreme, as having equal value to that of the immutable truths of the doctrine of faith. At present the authentic spiritual significance of the liturgy is not accessible to these people.

However, our liturgical texts can form the best means of providing access to the theological, spiritual and missionary message of the church, since they reflect the perfect teaching of twenty centuries of Christianity. By penetrating the significance of these texts, every Christian can gain a mass of indispensable knowledge in practically all spheres of church doctrine and tradition. That is why we are called seriously to reflect on the way in which the liturgy can be made more accessible to all.

Immutability of the faith and evolution of liturgical culture. In the church, there are some things which are eternal and some which are temporal. If the dogmas of the Orthodox faith which constitute the intangible foundation of the church remain immutable, the expression of these divine truths in the form of given cultural forms, including liturgical culture, has developed over the centuries. It was still developing at the beginning of our century. However, in the ex-USSR, in which the life of the church was oppressed by an atheistic power, this development became unthinkable, and as a result the process was so to speak interrupted in 1917.

Now this development will continue, but that calls for an indispensable effort to mobilize the collegial awareness of the church in its totality. We believe that we have to organize the liturgical life of the church in a spirit of collegiality, in such a way that it allows us to reactivate its education and missionary elements.

To this end, it seems to us useful to form a special synodical commission which will continue the work that the local council [of the Russian Orthodox Church] of 1917–1918 began in the hope of ordering liturgical practice, but which could not be completed. This commission could equally revise the translation of the liturgical texts, which was also begun in the past but never finished. In the perspective of the preparation of the final documents of the episcopal assembly I ask you to reflect on the value of the creation of such a commission and the organization of a central ecclesial structure charged with missionary action.

A contextual approach. In this connection, it is necessary to emphasize that today more than ever the mission of our church must be expressed through the most varied forms, and that it must implement an adequate approach, following the social categories to which our message is addressed.

Thus in the major industrialized urban centres, among other things the mission of the church includes a particular form of service and witness within the working-class world and the social and professional movements, and also among deprived persons who are victims of urbanization and modern technology.

The work of the church with young people constitutes another special sphere of missionary action, which includes the organization of liturgical celebrations and catechetical discussions with children and adolescents.

The missionary action of the church in the different spheres of the cultural world also faces difficult conditions which call for a specific approach. This should take account of the fact that a state of mind stamped by secularization and agnosticism prevails in these levels of post-Soviet society; they are influenced by ideas imported from outside which are alien, if not frankly hostile, to Orthodoxy.

The social involvement of the church. In the general context of the social, political and ethnic contradictions and conflicts which have appeared in the countries of the former USSR, problems linked to the involvement of the church in the social problems of the modern world and the role of Christianity in the construction of the nation have a quite particular missionary dimension.

The interest of our church in questions of economic policy, ecology and social justice also has an immediate missionary significance, as does our participation in the efforts of humankind as a whole to find solutions to these current problems. The same can be said for the involvement of our church in the fight for peace, in service among the poor and the oppressed, refugees, immigrants and the unemployed.

Creation of missionary structures. In these conditions it is vital to touch on the question of the creation of missionary structures at the level of each diocese, to speak of missionary work in the parishes, and to call for the involvement of our faithful in Christian witness and everyday *diaconia*, not only as an element of the personal commitment of parishioners but above all as a communal expression of 'the liturgy after the liturgy'.

On all these essential questions we must make proposals which will serve as points of reference for the missionary work to be done in the dioceses, parishes, monasteries and other ecclesial structures. The synodical commission for theology and the department of the Patriarchate responsible for religious education and catechesis must pay the greatest attention to the specific training of Orthodox missionaries. The future will show us what our possibilities, our perspectives and our limits are here, but nevertheless we must lay the foundation for this work now.

Working for the synthesis of a coherent Christian culture. Here we must be inspired by the teaching of the primitive church and use the rich experience of our missionary past. We must weigh up our current needs and possibilities, constantly remembering the difficult years of witness and suffering which we lived through during the post-revolutionary period. We must also work at the synthesis of a coherent Christian culture, a synthesis which will be the creative reflection of the absolute truth of Orthodoxy in an environment which is permanently changing.

The mistakes of the past, the inadequacy of our resources, the difficulties and the failures, must not trouble us. The hard period from which our church has just emerged and the new trials which it is undergoing today must be a school of rebirth and renewal for all of us.

The call to a new life. We must accept everything that our church and our people are experiencing today as a call from divine Providence to renounce our 'past existence, to renew us by a spiritual transformation of our understanding and to put on the new man' (Eph.4.22–25). 'But now we are discharged from the law, dead to that which held us captive, so that we do not serve under the old written code' (Rom.7.6), so that we too may walk 'in a new life' (Rom.6.4).

Only then will the Orthodox church, accomplishing its mission in society, again become as in times past a decisive spiritual factor in the history of the Orthodox people who are established on the territory of our different countries.

The Russian church, which has always preserved the Orthodox faith and brings the light of Christ to those who are near and those who are far off, is today experiencing a difficult period of internal restructuring in conditions which offer us numerous new possibilities while also presenting us with numerous new challenges.

Remain faithful to justice and love. May the words which I have just spoken be truly in accord with the word of the Lord who guides his church through joys and pains. May these words serve the peace, salvation and prosperity of the children of our church and our peoples. May they remove from our lives all the discords, temptations, divisions and obstacles which hinder our church in the accomplishment of its saving mission in the midst of the complex world of today. May they remain faithful to the divine justice and the commandment to love which our Lord and Saviour has given us. 'Through those who trust in You, O Lord, strengthen the Church that you gained through your precious blood' (Canon of the Feast of the Holy Encounter, hirmos of the third ode).

Notes

1. On 5 May 1995 Patriarch Aleksi and the Holy Synod of the Russian Orthodox Church published a communication on the occasion of the fiftieth anniversary of the end of the Second World War. It states, among other things, that 'the victory which we celebrate today is not just a historical event. It is something that is important for those of us who are alive today. "God is not in power but in truth", said the highly Orthodox prince Aleksandr Nevsky. The power of God was with the people because we were fighting for the truth and because the Lord saw the spirit of the people, who were united in defence of life and peace, in opposition to the atheistic and totalitarian ideology which was dominating the country at that time. Is this not perhaps an example in the light of which we can consider the numerous warlike conflicts, economic crises, the growth of criminality and the crisis of state power in which today's generations are living? The church believes and hopes that this time, too, the people will be able to join ranks with an aspiration to regenerate their power. It believes and hopes that the victory obtained half a century ago will become a model for coping with the difficulties which have to be overcome today, a model of liberation from the grave problems with which we are afflicted' (quoted from *Il Regno-Documenti*, 15/1995, 507).

2. '128 bishops of the Russian Orthodox Church met in plenary assembly between 29 November and 2 December 1994 at the Danilov Monastery in Moscow under the presidency of their primate, Patriarch Aleksi II. It was officially stated that the theme of this gathering, "Mission in the Contemporary World", gave rise to "serious discussions" both in plenary session and in working groups. With a missionary aim, the assembly approved the principle of making the liturgy accessible to the largest possible number of people. It also spoke in favour of the pursuit of theological dialogue with the other churches and Christian confessions and the continuation of the Russian church in the ecumenical organizations of which it is a member' (SOP 194/1995, 2–3).

3. Patriarch Aleksi's text is taken from the French translation published by SOP 194, January 1995, 30–3.

4. *Dilatentur spatia caritatis*, Augustine, *Sermo* 69.1 (PL 38, 440–1).

5. In his report, the patriarch provided numerous pieces of statistical and financial information. At present the Russian church comprises 15,985 churches on the territory of the former USSR (as opposed to 6,800 in 1988), 260 of them in Moscow itself (as opposed to around 40 in 1988), served by 12,841 priests and 1,402 deacons. 3 theological academies, 14 seminaries and a total of 47 schools ensure the training of 4,000 theologians, priests, catechists, chapel masters and iconographers. In addition, 2,000 are engaged in theological training by correspondence. 281 monastic communities exist or are in the course of formation. Materially the situation remains very precarious because of the economic and financial crisis. The income of the Patriarchate, for the past two and half years, has increased by more than 10 billion roubles (1 US dollar = 3,327 roubles at the official rate), and its expenses for the last 23 months have risen by 7.5 billion roubles, 54% attriibutable to the theological schools (SOP 194/ January 1995, 3).

Contributors

D. M. SHAKHOVSKOI is Professor at the Theological Institute of St Sergius in Paris, and Secretary of the Patriarchal Exarchate of Western Europe (Russian Orthodox Church).

EMMANUEL LANNE was born in Paris in 1923. He has been a Benedictine monk at the Monastery of Chèvetogne since 1946. He has taught Eastern theology, ecumenical theology and Eastern liturgy at Rome and Louvain (Louvain-la-Neuve). He is a former rector of the Greek College of St Athanasius in Rome, and a member and former vice-president of the Faith and Order Commission of the World Council of Churches, an advisor to the Pontifical Council of the Unity of Christians and the Congregation for the Eastern Churches, and director of the journal *Irénikon*. He has written on the Coptic liturgy, Eastern theology and ecumenism.

Address: Monastère de la Sainte Croix, B – 5590 Chèvetogne, Belgium.

VLADIMIR KOTELNIKOV was born in Omsk in 1947. He completed his studies at the Pedagogical Institute of Leningrad with a doctoral thesis on *I.V.Kireeevsky i ego vremya*, 1980, and a habilitation thesis on *Pravoslavie v tvorchestve russkikh pisatelei*, 1994. He is a member of the Institute of Russian Literature of the Academy of Russian Science, and lectures at the Russian State University of Education. He has lectured at the Universities of Turin and Warsaw. Recent publications include *Pravoslavnaya asketika i russyaja literatura*, St Petersburg 1994 and numerous articles.

Address: nab.Makarova 4, IRLI Pushkinsky Dom, 199034 St Petersburg, Russia.

ALEKSI I. OSIPOV was born in 1938. He is a professor and doctor of theology. In 1963 he completed his studies at the Theological Academy in Moscow, gaining first a licenciate and then a doctorate there. He immediately began teaching at the Academy and was appointed professor in 1975. He is currently a member of various theological commissions of the Russian Orthodox Church and has taken part in numerous bilateral colloquia, among them dialogues between the International Theological Commission and both the Lutherans and the Faith and Order Commission of the WCC. He has also taken part in numerous inter-confessional meetings.

Address: Theological Academy, Moscow Moskoskaya Duchovnaya Akademiya, Troice-Serg Laura-Sergiev Posad, Moscow Oblas, Russia.

ADRIANO ROCCUCCI was born in 1962 and graduated in history at the University of Rome 'La Sapienza'. He has a doctorate in contemporary history and is engaged in post-doctoral research at the Department of Historical Studies from the Middle Ages to the Present Day at the Third University of Rome. His field of research is the anti- religious policy of the Soviets and the history of the Russian Orthodox Church in the Soviet period.

Address: Largo G.Belloni 4, 00191 Rome, Italy.

NICOLAS LOSSKY is Professor of Britannic Civilization at the University of Paris X, Professor of Church History at the Orthodox Theological Institude of St Sergius in Paris, Director of the Institut Supérieur d'Études Oecumeniques at the Institut Catholique in Pais and a member of the Standing Comittee of the Faith and Order Commission of the World Council of Churches. He is the author of *Lancelot Andrewes (1555–1626), the Preacher: The Origin of the Mystical Theology of the Church of England*, Oxford 1991, and co-editor of the *Dictionary of the Ecumenical Movement*, Geneva 1991.

Address: Université de Paris X, 66 rue d'Hautpoul, 75019 Paris, France.

FRANZ KÖNIG was born in Rabenstein, Austria, in 1905. He was ordained priest in 1933, elected bishop in 1952, and became Archbishop of Vienna in 1956 and Cardinal in December 1958. He has been archbishop emeritus since 1985. He played a pioneering role in churches beyond the 'Iron Curtain', and took an active part in Vatican II and in the conclaves of 1963 and 1978. He has presided over the institution of the Secretariat for Non-Believers. His publications include *Christus und die Religionen der Erde* (3 vols), Vienna 1951; *Die Konzilsidee von Konstanz bis Vatikanum II*, Cologne 1965; and, on his ecumenical work, *Veritati in caritate*, Innsbruck 1981.

Address: Wollzeile 2, 1010 Vienna, Austria.

ALBERTO MELLONI was born at Reggio Emilia on 6 January 1959, is a member of the staff of the Institute for Religious Sciences in Bologna and teaches at Rome University III. He has published studies on the history of mediaeval canon law, the councils, and the church in modern times. He has also edited sources and published studies on John XXIII and is editor of the Italian edition of the *History of the Second Vatican Council*, directed by G.Alberigo; he also edited the publication of the *Notes quotidiennes au Concile* by M.-D.Chenu, Paris 1995, and he organized the colloquium 'Vatican II at Moscow', on the Russian and Soviet participation in the Council, the proceedings of which are in preparation in Louvain and Moscow.

Address: Via Elba 33, I 42100 Reggio Emilia, Italy.

GEORGY ZYABLITSEV was born in 1955 and gained a licenciate in theology in 1986. Since 1990 he has worked in the Department of Foreign Affairs of the Moscow Patriarchate, in the area of relations with the Catholic Church. He was ordained priest by Kirill, Metropolitan of Smolensk and Kaliningrad, in 1993. He has written much on theology and taken part in bilateral discussions between the Russian Orthodox Church and the Roman Catholic Church.

Address: Department of Foreign Affairs, Danilov Wall 22, 113191 Moscow, Russia.

ÉTIENNE FOUILLOUX was born in Paris in 1941; he studied history at the École normale supérieure, Saint Cloud, and the Sorbonne; he graduated in history in 1965 and gained a doctorate in letters in 1980. He taught history at the University of Nanterre (1969–1981) and then became Professor of Contemporary History at the Universities of Caen (1981–1990) and Lyon (since 1990). His publications include: *Les catholiques et l'unité chrétienne du XIXe au XXe siècle. Itinéraires européens d'expression française*, Paris 1982; *Au coeur du XXe siècle religieux,* Paris 1993; *Yves de Montcheuil, philosophe et théologien jésuite (1900–1944)*, Paris 1995; *La collection 'Sources chrétiennes'. Editer les Pères de l'Église au XXe siècle*, Paris 1995.

Address: 10, avenue Salvador Allende, 69100 Villeurbanne, France.

VITALY BOROVOI, protopresbyter and professor, was born in Byelorussia in 1916. He studied at the seminary of Vilnius (1928–1936) and the theological faculty of the University of Warsaw (1936–1939), gaining a doctorate in theology, was ordained in 1943, and then became rector of the seminary in Minsk, where he also taught church history. From 1954 to 1962 he was professor of early church history at the seminary of St Petersburg. He was an observer at the Second Vatican Council, and represented the Russian Orthodox Church at the WCC from 1969, being Vice-President of the Faith and Order Commission up to 1972. From 1972 to 1995 he taught Byzantinology and Western church history at the Theological Academy of Moscow and is at present a consultant to the Department of Foreign Affairs of the Moscow Patriarchate.

Address: Department of Foreign Affairs, Danilov Wall 22, 113191 Moscow, Russia.

GIUSEPPE ALBERIGO was born in Varese in 1926 and since 1967 has been Professor of Church History in the faculty of political sciences in the University of Bologna. He is secretary of the Institute of Religious Sciences, Bologna. Publications include: *I vescovi italiani al concilio di Trento*, 1959; *Lo sviluppo della dottrina sui poteri nella Chiesa universale*, 1964; *Cardinalato e collegialità*, 1969; *Chiesa conciliare*, 1981; *Legge e Vangelo*, 1972; *Indices verborum et locutionum decretorum concilii Vaticani II* (8 vols); *Synopsis historica della* Lumen gentium, 1975; *Giovanni XXIII, Profezia nella fedeltà*, 1978; *Fede, Tradizione, Profezia*, 1984; *La Chiesa nella Storia*, 1989; *Nostalgie di unità*, 1989. He has also edited *Conciliorum Oecumenicorum Decreta*, ^{3}1973 and contributed to many historial and theological journals. He is editor of the quarterly review *Cristianesimo nella Storia*.

Address: Via G.Mazzini 82, I-40138, Bologna, Italy.

To the Readers of *Concilium*

A Statement from the Foundation

For more than thirty years the editors and publishers of *Concilium* have tried to provide you with reliable information and critical reflection from every area of theology. The journal came into being as a result of the spirit of renewal evident at the Second Vatican Council and in the future too will seek, through the inspiration of that spirit, to stimulate new thought and practice in the church, among the religions and in world societies and cultures. *Concilium* means to remain faithful to its global perspectives and invites theologians from all over the world to share in its work.

In order to do even more justice to *Concilium*'s claim to global theological perspectives, its editors and publishers have decided on the following improvements to *Concilium* from the first issue in 1997.

1. The topics of the individual issues of *Concilium* will no longer be connected directly to the traditional theological disciplines, but will be discussed from a variety of theological perspectives. This will guarantee a broader and more open theological discussion of urgent contemporary questions in the church and the world.

2. The editors of *Concilium* reaffirm their commitment to reflect appropriately on all the important theological problem areas, and at the same time to involve a large number of younger theologians.

3. To meet the changed reading habits of our time, *Concilium* will appear five times a year instead of six. The annual cycle of subject areas covered will comprise:

- Christian faith
- Ethics and lifestyle
- Church and community, ecumenism, structures and communications
- Religious experience, religious movements and religious indifference
- Global perspectives, feminist theology and liberation theology.

Concilium seeks to continue to reach readers of all generations who are interested in the renewal of Christian faith in today's world and who seek reliable and critical information on current developments – as for example the rediscovery of the God of Jesus Christ in the various cultural contexts of our world; local and global renewal movements in the church; recent developments in the ecumenical sphere; the equality of men and women; the struggle for justice among the nations; the dialogue between the religions; ethical conflicts; and new ways of mutual understanding and collaboration.

We thank you for your interest in *Concilium* and at the same time would ask you to support the editorial board of *Concilium* with your suggestions and your criticisms.

Members of the Board of Directors

Foundation

Anton van den Boogard	President	Nijmegen	The Netherlands
Paul Brand	Secretary	Ankeveen	The Netherlands
Werner Jeanrond		Lund	Sweden
Dietmar Mieth		Tübingen	Germany
Christoph Theobald SJ		Paris	France

Founders

Anton van den Boogaard — Nijmegen — The Netherlands
Paul Brand — Ankeveen — The Netherlands
Yves Congar OP† — Paris — France
Hans Küng — Tübingen — Germany
Johann Baptist Metz — Vienna — Austria
Karl Rahner SJ† — Innsbruck — Austria
Edward Schillebeeckx OP — Nijmegen — The Netherlands

Directors-Counsellors

José Oscar Beozzo — São Paolo — Brazil
Virgil Elizondo — San Antonio, TX — USA
Seán Freyne — Dublin — Ireland
Hermann Häring — Nijmegen — The Netherlands
Maureen Junker-Kenny — Dublin — Ireland
Werner Jeanrond — Lund — Sweden
François Kabasele Lumbala — Mbuji Mayi — Zaire
Karl-Josef Kuschel — Tübingen — Germany
Nicholas Lash — Cambridge — Great Britain
Dietmar Mieth — Tübingen — Germany
John Panagnopoulos — Athens — Greece
Giuseppe Ruggieri — Catania — Italy
Elisabeth Schüssler Fiorenza — Cambridge, MA — USA
Christoph Theobald SJ — Paris — France
Miklós Tomka — Budapest — Hungary
David Tracy — Chicago, IL — USA
Marciano Vidal CSSR — Madrid — Spain
Felix Wilfred — Madras — India
Ellen van Wolde — Tilburg — The Netherlands

General Secretariat: Prins Bernardstraat 2, 6521 A B Nijmegen, The Netherlands
Manager: Mrs E. C. Duindam-Deckers

Members of the Advisory Committee for Church History

Directors

Giuseppe Alberigo	Bologna	Italy
José Oscar Beozzo	São Paulo SP	Brazil

Members

Arnold Angenendt	Münster	Germany
Roger Aubert	Louvain-la-Neuve	Belgium
Victor Conzemius	Lucerne	Switzerland
Enrique Dussel	Mexico City	Mexico
Gerald P. Fogarty	Charlottesville, VA	USA
Etienne Fouilloux	Lyons	France
Matthijs Lamberigts	Louvain	Belgium
Armando Lampe	Chemutal	Mexico
Ng. Lee-Ming	Hong Kong	Hong Kong
Giacomo Martina SJ	Rome	Italy
Alberto Melloni	Bologna	Italy
David Mungello	Cedar Rapids, Iowa	USA
Bernard Plongeron	Paris	France
Emile Poulat	Paris	France
Peter Raedts	Nijmegen	The Netherlands
Hilari Raguer	Montserrat	Spain
Helga Robinson-Hammerstein	Dublin	Ireland
Claude Soetens	Louvain-La-Neuve	Belgium
Tetonio de Souza SJ	Goa	India
Brian Tierney	Ithaca, NY	Etats-Unis
John Mary Waliggo	Kampala	Uganda
Anton G. Weiler	Nijmegen	The Netherlands

Concilium Subscription Information - outside North America

Individual Annual Subscription (five issues): £25.00
Institution Annual Subscription (five issues): £35.00
Airmail subscriptions: add £10.00
Individual issues: £8.95 each

New subscribers please return this form:
for a two-year subscription, double the appropriate rate

(for individuals)   £25.00   (1/2 years)   . . . .

(for institutions)   £35.00   (1/2 years)   . . . .

Airmail postage
outside Europe +£10.00   (1/2 years)   . . . .

                                         Total   . . . .

I wish to subscribe for one/two years as an individual/institution
(delete as appropriate)

Name/Institution . . . .

Address . . . .

. . . .

. . . .

I enclose a cheque for . . . . payable to SCM Press Ltd

Please charge my Access/Visa/Mastercard no. . . . .

Signature . . . . Expiry Date . . . .

Please return this form to:
SCM PRESS LTD 9 - 17 St Albans Place   London   N1 0NX

CONCILIUM

The Theological Journal of the 1990s

Now available from Orbis Books

Founded in 1965 and published five times a year, *Concilium* is a world-wide journal of theology. Its editors and essayists encompass a veritable 'who's who' of theological scholars. Not only the greatest names in Catholic theology, but also exciting new voices from every part of the world, have written for this unique journal.

Concilium exists to promote theological discussion in the spirit of Vatican II, out of which it was born. It is a catholic journal in the widest sense: rooted firmly in the Catholic heritage, open to other Christian traditions and the world's faiths. Each issue of *Concilium* focusses on a theme of crucial importance and the widest possible concern for our time. With contributions from Asia, Africa, North and South America and Europe, *Concilium* truly reflects the multiple facets of the world church.

Now available from Orbis Books, *Concilium* will continue to focus theological debate and to challenge scholars and students alike.

Please enter my subscription to **Concilium** 1997/1-6
[ ] individual US$60.00   [ ] institutional US$75.00

Please send the following back issues at US$15.00 each

1996 . . . . 1995 . . . .
1994 . . . . 1993 . . . .
1992 . . . . 1991 . . . .

[ ] MC/Visa . . . . . . / . . . . . . / . . . . . . / . . . . . Expires . . . .
[ ] Check (payable to Orbis Books)

Name/Institution . . . .
Address . . . .
City/State/Zip . . . .
Telephone . . . .

Send order and payment to:
Orbis Books, Box 302, Maryknoll, NY 10545-0302 USA